Problem Oriented
Programming Languages

Problem 4.6.6.6
Programming Language

Problem Oriented Programming Languages

Professor Dr. rer. nat. Hans Jürgen Schneider
Universität Erlangen-Nürnberg, Germany

Translated by
Valerie H. Cottrell with the assistance of
Wendy J. Pitkin

JOHN WILEY & SONS
Chichester · New York · Brisbane · Toronto · Singapore

Originally published under the title Problemorientierte
Programmiersprachen by H.J. Schneider.
© B.G. Teubner, Stuttgart 1981.

This edition is published by permission of Verlag B.G. Teubner, Stuttgart, and is the sole
authorized English translation of the original German edition.

Library of Congress Cataloging in Publication Data:

Schneider, Hans Jürgen, 1937–
    Problem oriented programming languages.
    Translation of: Problemorientierte Programmierspra-
chen.
    Includes bibliographical references and index.
    1. Programming languages (Electronic computers)
I. Title.
QA76.7.S3513   1984   001.64'24   83-16688

ISBN 0 471 90111 3

British Library Cataloguing in Publication Data:

Schneider, Hans Jürgen
    Problem oriented programming languages.
    1. Programming languages (Electronic computers)
    2. Electronic digital computers—Programming
    I. Title   I. Problemorientierte
Programmiersprachen. *English*.
001.64'24   QA76.7

ISBN 0 471 90111 3

Typeset by MHL Typesetting Ltd., Coventry
Printed in Great Britain at the Pitman Press Ltd., Bath, Avon.

Contents

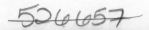

Preface

Problem oriented programming languages were initially developed in order to formulate machine possibilities more conveniently. FORTRAN II is a typical representative of this period. Later, the importance of structuring became apparent: ALGOL 60 placed emphasis on the structure of algorithms, COBOL on that of data. Several hundred programming languages were based on and developed alongside these classic examples.

For a long time, it seemed as though a programmer (the term is used as a simplified description of anyone involved with programming languages) would never have to relearn anything, as more attention was paid to existing program libraries than to experiments with new languages. It is only in the last few years that there has been both a total change of direction in some quarters and further development of older languages in the light of recent progress. The question is, does the programmer have to relearn programming? The answer is essentially negative, but programming languages are often basically different both in concept as well as in the resultant terminology.

This book attempts to provide a uniform description of the most widely used problem oriented programming languages plus those from which new trends have emerged or could emerge in the future. This may facilitate transfer from one language to another by clarifying some of the analogies and differences. It also gives some insight into languages other than those which are of direct use. Many a concept provided in more recent programming languages can be used as a programming technique in a more established language and thereby improve the quality of both program and programmer alike.

Programming languages are a recursive affair: one language structure often requires knowledge of all the others in order to be understood. In fact, there is no point at which one can begin without having to make certain assumptions. Textbooks offer help in the main by beginning with a simplified explanation and then following up each aspect in more detail. This book, however, is not a textbook on programming as such. It is assumed that the reader is thoroughly conversant with at least one problem oriented programming language and because of this will readily grasp many a formulation based on language structures covered in a later part of the book. However, some points will still remain obscure, depending on which languages he is familiar with.

There is an immense amount of literature published on programming languages and, for this reason, only review or historically relevant material has been mentioned.† However, one objective has been to counter a bad habit which is common throughout computer science literature—the more remote publications, for example technical reports from universities and firms which are often difficult for the *average reader* to obtain, have been omitted.

Finally, I would like to thank my colleagues Prof. Dr. M. Nagl (Osnabrück University) and Prof. Dr. W. Stucky (Karlsruhe University) for all their work in sifting through the material assembled for the book and the valuable advice and ideas emerging from it.

Erlangen   H. J. SCHNEIDER

---

† In translating this book, the list of references was completed by adding some English textbooks on several programming languages.

1
Concepts

1.1 Language

Language is a means of communication. This applies to programming languages just as much as to the so-called natural ones. A look at the history of programming will show that communication between the programmer† and the digital computer (albeit very one-sided) played a significant role during the early development stages: the language had to be able to describe algorithms. Later as the documentation came to the fore communication between the various people involved with the program became more important; thus the emphasis was more on the accurate and legible description of algorithms. As programming languages ripened, self-communication was the keynote: the programmer's earliest thoughts had to be recorded. Formulations which are written down serve as the basis for future revision, modification and correction of original ideas. In the hands of a programmer, a programming language is a tool which has a decisive influence on the quality of the end product, i.e. the program. The language should support the process of developing algorithms. Wegner (1979) described it as follows: 'Programming languages, like natural languages, have a fundamental impact on our thought processes. Languages with names such as Pascal and Euclid reflect the realization of their designers that languages should facilitate thought processes of mathematical problem-solving.'

The Anglo-Austrian philosopher Wittgenstein was originally of the opinion that the structure of a language depended on the structure of real life. However, much later he became convinced that the reverse was true, that our language determines our view of reality (Pears, 1971). When applied to the field of programming languages, this means that the structure of the programming

---

† The word programmer is used throughout to describe anyone working with a program.

language with which the programmer is familiar will affect the way in which he sees the algorithms to be described. Different languages will, therefore, give different views and this can lead to misunderstandings. Zemanek (1971) made the following remark on the subject: 'The problem is not the competition between ALGOL, PL/I and other constructed languages used in programming—if it were, we could manage with interpreters and translators. The real problem is that there is confusion in the thought processes and methods of description.'

Naur (1975) wrote a remarkable paper on the differences and similarities between programming and natural languages. One significant difference is that the former are written down and the latter are used mainly in the spoken form. So, if programming language developers are interested in acceptance of their products, they can learn something from the way natural language has evolved: in a nutshell, it reflects the influence of millions of individuals over the centuries. One of the salient features to emerge is the preference for the shorter, more regular, and less numerous forms.

1.2 Algorithms

Programming languages are used to describe algorithms. By this we mean a set of rules for performing a calculation which satisfy the following conditions: (1) The description must be complete. (2) The description must be unequivocal. (3) The specification described must be effective.

The concept of complete implies that the algorithm can only consist of a finite number of steps and requires only a finite number of characters to describe it. However, the definition does not specify the form in which the individual steps are described nor the characters used for the purpose. Unequivocal means that the effect of each individual step is clearly laid down and that the exact sequence of steps is also made plain. Effective† means that the execution of each individual step should take only a finite amount of time, i.e. does actually come to an end. This ensures that the next step can be started but not necessarily that the algorithm as a whole will come to a halt.

An algorithm does not terminate if and only if an infinite number of steps are to be carried out.

However, this is not an inherent property of the algorithm and may well depend on the parameters involved. The following algorithm, used to describe a factorial function, can be taken as an example:

$$n! = n \times (n-1) \times (n-2)...2 \times 1$$

This can be transposed to a self-evident programming language and then appears as follows:

---

† 'Effective' should not be confused with 'efficient': the former means that the plan can be implemented, the latter that it requires minimum resources of either time or space .

factorial(n) =
 IF *n* = *0 THEN 1*
  *ELSE n * factorial(n – 1)*
 END IF.

This algorithm terminates if and only if $n \geqslant 0$ initially.

The theory of computability has shown that not all mathematically well-defined functions are computable. This means that we cannot formulate an algorithm which will supply the function values under arbitrarily chosen parameters. One non-computable function relevant to the sphere of programming is as follows: $t(p,d)$ requires a program as its first parameter and the program's data as its second. The function value of $t(p,d)$ is exactly *1* when program *p* finishes with data *d*, and otherwise it is *0*. The fact that this function is non-computational means that there can be no program which checks others for the presence of continuous loops (non-decidability of the halting problem). This makes it all the more important for a good programming language not only to exclude the possibility of hidden continuous loops but also to reveal any critical points.

The definition of an algorithm given here represents the sequential process. This means that each individual step must be fully complete before the next one can begin, and that its execution does not depend on conditions outside the range of the algorithm. However, these types of influences do occur during the synchronization of processes operating in parallel. Thus, it could happen that none of the processes proceed even though none have reached the end (system deadlock). This is another aspect of the halting problem.

1.3 Language levels

A language with which algorithms can be formulated is called an algorithmic language.

An algorithmic language is a system of a finite number of characters and a finite number of rules in which the latter in some way establishes the character sequences to describe computable functions. It is called universal if it is capable of describing all computable functions.

Thus, algorithmic language is a special version of formal language, in which there is a selection of acceptable character sequences but where no meaning is actually ascribed to them. An algorithmic language becomes a programming language when the character sequence can be processed by a digital computer. This definition is a function of time as it depends upon the potential of available input devices and the level of translation technique attained. The 'Plankalkül' of Zuse (1949, 1959) (described in up-to-date terms by Bauer and Wössner, (1972)) is an example of an algorithmic language which has had no significance as a programming language, although it is basically suitable for this purpose.

One way in which algorithmic languages differ from each other is in the extent to which their means of expression is suited to the potential of specific

4

digital computers. According to DIN 44300,† there are three levels of language: machine language, machine oriented language and problem oriented language.

A machine language is a programming language whose only statements for writing down an algorithm are in the form of direct orders to the digital computer.

These languages are not easy to work with, as the programmer needs not only to master the machine structure, but also the internal representation of all information.

A programming language is said to be machine oriented if its statements are of the same or similar structure to the instructions for a specific computer.

They differ from machine languages in that they use decimal numbers, mnemonic symbols for operations, symbolic addresses, *macro* and *pseudo* instructions, etc. Macro instructions cannot generally be carried out by one machine instruction. They are available for such things as servicing, but can also be defined by the programmer himself. Pseudo instructions do not correspond to any instructions in the translated program; they are instructions to the translator and are used for such purposes as the reservation of storage locations for data or control of translation protocol.

This book is dedicated to the highest of the three language levels:

A programming language is problem oriented if it is capable of dealing with algorithms from a specific area of application independent of any particular type of computer, and if it is modelled on a method of speech or writing normally used in this problem area.

Its emphasis on problems makes this type of language especially suitable for documentation purposes. Languages designed for the techno-scientific market must allow suitable formulation of arithmetic expressions or iterations, those designed for commercial and administrative purposes must incorporate language elements which can cope with data files and tabulations.† Thus, primitive objects and actions form one essential part of a problem-oriented programming language, and the rules on how to derive composed objects (e.g. arrays, files) from primitive ones, plus expressions derived from primitive actions, form the other. Around this central concept, which is basically responsible for determining the application range of the language, lies the sphere of program construction. This contains control structures for describing the control flow, and language structures for defining program parts more independently of each other (procedures, modules, processes). In such a way, the structure of executable objects is dealt with at this level. Any change of these forms part of the so-called dialogue language (Kupka and Wilsing (1975) and Schneider (1980) give a comparison between some dialogue languages); hence, the outside layer is known as the dialogue layer.

There are two types of problem oriented languages between which we must differentiate: procedural languages and very high-level languages. On further

---

† DIN 44300 corresponds to international standard ISO 2382.
† Both types are required for industrial management projects based on mathematical models.

consideration, only the procedural languages are seen to be algorithmic languages, since description of the algorithm is their focal point. On the other hand, very high-level languages allow description of the problem, and the algorithm is then derived mechanically from it. It is not the object of this book to give a detailed study of these languages; problems and proposed solutions are described in a symposium paper by Leavenworth (1974).

1.4 Lines of development

The individual can no longer be given just an approximate view of all problem oriented programming languages. Even a summary must be restricted to the most important items, and the degree of importance attached to one or the other is always coloured by personal bias. Sammet's roster, which is regularly updated, is one important guideline; she omits languages which are implemented for one specific machine only or those used by the inventor alone. The most up-to-date list available at the time of publication was for 1976 – 7 (Sammet 1978a). This roster, however, has two very important drawbacks. Firstly, the minimum limits set before a language is accepted are too low. Secondly, the list is confined to languages used in the USA, even though European developments have made a great contribution to the systematic investigation of the structure of problem oriented programming languages, as shown by the widespread use of PASCAL and the success of a mainly European group in the development of ADA.

A comparison of Sammet's rosters shows that the stormy period through which programming languages went during the 1960s is now rather more settled: 171 languages were listed for 1973, 167 for 1975 and 166 for 1977. One remarkable point is that of the 33 languages which appeared in the 1973 index for the first time, five were omitted from the following index and a further eight from the 1977 one. Schnupp (1978) has put forward various arguements to explain this non-movement of accepted languages.

Fig. 1.1 shows a small section from the genealogy of programming languages. Three aspects should be considered: (1) the most widely used languages all have a predecessor which gained no long-term acceptance in itself, (2) all widely used languages have lived through a development period, and (3) the various languages have all influenced each other during their development period; thus, even experimental languages which have not found acceptance themselves have been instrumental in stimulating the development of others.

The history of programming languages can be divided up into three phases as Sammet (1972) has described.

(1) 1952 – 1958   seed time
(2) 1958 – 1960   blossom time
(3) 1960 onwards   ripening time

Phase (1) was characterized by the desire to work out a more convenient formulation of machine possibilities. Arithmetic expressions and a simple iteration were the only available linguistic aids. FORTRAN II is one typical representative of this period. Phase (2) recognized the importance of structure. ALGOL

6

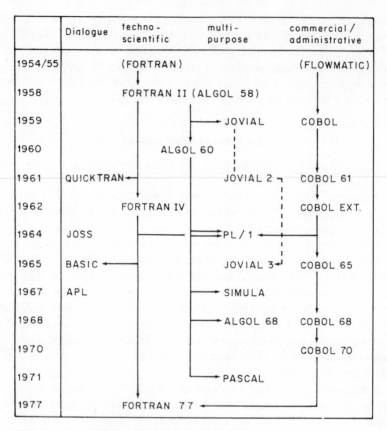

Fig. 1.1   Development of programming languages.

60 emphasizes algorithm structuring and COBOL is more concerned with data structuring. A basic analysis of the advantages and disadvantages of specific concepts marked the beginning of phase (3). The most well-known example of this analysis is the GOTO controversy (Denning (1974) gives the pros and cons of this). There is some reason to believe that harvest time has arrived meanwhile. Weicker (1978) has given a comprehensive survey of some of the more modern developments (PASCAL, LIS, EUCLID, CLU, ALPHARD, MODULA, ADA[†]). Apart from any possible acceptance of these languages, the concepts embodied in them are important stepping stones for the future development of classical languages (Fig. 1.2).

1.5 Syntax, semantics, pragmatics

When defining what is understood by algorithmic language, two aspects have already emerged to assist in its characterization: (1) Which character sequences are the correctly constructed ones within the definition of this language? (2) Which computable function is described by a particular character sequence?

---

† ADA is a registered trademark of the US Government – ADA Joint Program Office.

Language	New aspect
FLOWMATIC	commercial applications
FORTRAN	techno-scientific applications
IPL	list processing
COMIT	character string processing
APT	special application range
COBOL	universally accepted language definition
JOVIAL	not restricted to one problem area, compiler written in the language
ALGOL 60	formal syntax definition
GPSS	simulation
LISP	functional programming
FORMAC	formula manipulation
JOSS	interactive language
APL	very high-level operators
SIMULA	coroutines
PASCAL	bootstrappable compilers
LIS	formulatable implementation data
EUCLID	verification support
CLU	abstract data types

Fig. 1.2 Milestones in the development of programming languages. Many aspects were developed simultaneously at different locations.

These two aspects are known as syntax and semantics respectively. A third aspect is pragmatics. (In accordance with an inaccurate but fully accepted language usage, these concepts are used both for investigating the object and for the object itself.) The American philologist Morris (1938, 1955) put these ideas into a formal framework, the essence of which is as follows.

Pragmatics deals with the origin, the use, and the effect of characters within the environment in which they occur (the relationship between characters and those who have to understand them). Semantics deals with the meaning of characters (the relationship between characters and the objects to which they are applicable). Syntax deals with the combination potential of characters without regard to their special meaning or relevance to the environment (the relationship between one character and another).

When these concepts are applied to the field of programming languages, syntax covers the regulations governing correct program structure. For example, it establishes how language elements are composed, in which sequence the constituent parts appear, and which separation signs are required. This area is by far the best formalized one and it will be covered in more detail in the next chapter.

Semantics researches the meaning of the program. It controls the effect of individual or composite language elements and the differences in meaning resulting from the context in which an element is used. Various methods giving a more formal specification of semantics are to be found in the literature. In the case of operational methods, a number of variables are assumed for a formal non-existent machine; the change of state caused by an operation defines its meaning. The most important advantage of this method, according to Guttag

(1977), is that programmers find it easier to grasp, as it does in fact involve programming to some extent. On the other hand, it favours implementation details which are frequently unnecessary. In the case of axiomatic methods, a set of relations are given combining the operations (without consideration of implementation). This algebra-based method is also the foundation for the concept of object type in the classical programming language.

The boundary between syntax and semantics is difficult to define. The language definitions of ALGOL 60, in which all aspects of language which were difficult or impossible to formally define at the time were put into the 'semantics' category, have played a significant part in creating misunderstanding (Naur *et al.*, 1963). For example, the condition that the number of subscripts must agree with the number of bound pairs in the related array declaration must be seen as a syntactic and not a semantic rule.

Algorithmic languages involve two basically different types of user—man and machine. For this reason, pragmatics can be viewed in two different ways—from a human and from a mechanical standpoint (Zemanek, 1966).

As regards mechanical pragmatics, the main objects are the question of language translatability, the demands made on the operating system, or the dependence on the properties of a specific computer family. The question of translatability includes ascertaining whether the translation process may be leading down a blind alley, which controls on translation time can be used, and whether an efficient machine program can be produced. Explicit or implicit aids for storage, data, and process administration are all points which are of significance with respect to the operating system. Finally, when designing a language, it is important to know which type of language constructions correspond directly to the capabilities of the available computer, or which computer properties would facilitate implementation and thus should become the objective of new computer development.

When dealing with human pragmatics, relationships to the human operator and to the area of application can be considered. Reading, learning, and teaching algorithmic languages are psychological problems which affect the success of a language just as much as technical details do. Questions such as which type of loops are available and whether recursive procedures are provided belong in this category. Also included are investigations into how advanced objects and actions are composed out of the more simple ones, and what form the resultant program structure will take. To date there has been very little systematic research carried out in this sphere. Brooks (1980) has recently considered several methodology problems. The differences in ways of speaking, and the variation in the data structures and operations required show how much influence the prospective area of application has. The objective of this book is to consider only languages which are not too closely tied up with one area of application. Topics such as data structuring and character string or list processing will be covered since they occur in many areas of use. However, languages developed specifically for problems involving machine tool control, computer-assisted teaching, artificial intelligence, etc. have been omitted as they fall outside the present scope.

2

Syntax

We now turn to syntax, dealing with the question as to which sequence of individual symbols describes a computable function in a specific programming language and is thus permissible, and which sequence of individual symbols is not acceptable. The former is often known as a correct string.[†] The concept of a value assignment as understood by most programming languages can be defined in a non-formal manner as follows: 'a value assignment consists of a variable, an assignment operator, and an expression, which must occur in that order. Many misunderstandings between authors and users of a programming language can be avoided if such definitions are replaced by formulae, especially when explaining examples which are more extensive and complex than the value assignment.

Thus, formal means for providing a syntactic description of programming languages were developed at a very early stage. The ALGOL family of languages, which use the combinatorial systems well known in the field of mathematics, have made the greatest contribution. As far back as the ALGOL 60 development period, Backus (1959) and Naur *et al.* (1960) proposed a formalism for describing syntax, known nowadays as the Backus-Naur-form (BNF).[‡] This formalism now incorporates some simplifications, and has become generally accepted. It can be readily transposed to a graphic representation (syntax diagram) which is also very popular in view of its clarity, even though no formal means are incorporated.

However, there are difficulties involved in formulating the syntactic rules for a programming language and leaving no gaps. Examples of this were given in section 1.5 when describing the boundary between syntax and semantics. Van

---

[†] Correctness relates to form only, in this case; whether or not the string describes the calculation intended by the programmer belongs to the field of semantics.

[‡] The literature also refers to a 'Backus Normal Form' but it is not clear what is meant by the term 'normal'.

Wijngaarden *et al.* (1969) based the development of ALGOL 68 on an extension of the Backus-Naur form (two-level grammar) and this can be used to describe many connections which cannot be expressed in the BNF (the example given in section 1.5 related to subscripts belongs in this category). Details of this extended form will not, however, be discussed at this point.

2.1 Backus-Naur form

The specification of the form of the value assignment, which has already been described in prose form, will now be noted in a more formal way using the actual simplified version of the Backus-Naur-form:

(1) *value assignment* :: = *variable* : = *expression*

The symbol :: = stands for 'is defined as'. It separates the notion to be described (left-hand side) from the definition (right-hand side). This example reveals a problem which always occurs when a notion is made up of several words; it is not clear whether the notion is a single element or made up of a sequence of several independent units. If the words are combined to form a notion, this is made clear by underlining the space between the words as shown in the following example. Once a notion has been defined, it can then be used in other rules pertaining to the language definition as a known factor:

(2)   *simple_statement* :: = *value_assignment* | *goto_statement*
          | *empty_statement* | *procedure_statement*

This rule shows that there are four different types of simple statement; alternatives are always separated from each other by a vertical line in the examples. In contrast to our simple example, some or all of the alternatives may consist of more than just a single component:

(3) *expression* :: = *term* | *expression* + *term* | *expression* - *term*

The definition scheme outlined here is a metalanguage by means of which a language can be discussed. Hence a difference must be made between the metalanguage symbols† and those of the language under consideration. In the three example rules, : = , + and − are symbols belonging to the language under review, in this case that of ALGOL 60. All other symbols belong to the metalanguage: they do not occur in an ALGOL 60 program. However, :: = and | are metalanguage symbols with fixed meaning; the language definition must contain at least one defining rule for each further non-specified symbol. To establish possible value assignment forms in ALGOL 60, rule (1) is used as a basis:

   variable : = *expression*

If the metalanguage symbol *expression* is replaced by the second alternative in rule (3), for example, the result is

   variable : = *expression* + *term*

and the first alternative of rule (3) can subsequently be used:

   variable : = *term* + *term*

This substitution process could then be continued with the symbols *variable* and *term*. It terminates when only symbols of the language under review are

---

† Use of the concepts 'symbol' and 'character' is in accordance with DIN 44300.

present. Thus the symbols of the metalanguage are called non-terminal symbols and those of the defined language are called terminal symbols.

As there is frequently a choice of various alternatives, generally several terminal symbol series can be derived from a non-terminal symbol.† If the notion under review occurs again on the right-hand side (recursion) as in example (3), then an infinite number of symbol sequences are generated due to the fact that the same non-terminal symbol is used any number of times and thus creates new symbols around it: example (3) defines expressions which consist of any number of terms. The substitution process comes to an end because an alternative exists in which the symbol under consideration no longer occurs. (In addition to this direct recursion, there is an indirect version in which the symbol to be defined re-appears after several substitution stages; this is the case for the symbol *expression* in Fig. 2.1.)

(1)   *block* ::= *BEGIN* { *declaration;* } * *statement__sequence END*
(2)   *statement__sequence* ::= *statement* { *; statement* } *
(3)   *statement* ::= { *label:* } * { *unconditional__statement* |
      conditional__statement | *loop* }
(4)   *unconditional__statement* ::= *simple__statement* | *block*
(5)   *simple__statement* ::= *value__assignment* | *goto__statement*
      | *empty__statement* | *procedure__statement*
(6)   *value__assignment* ::= { *left__side* := } + *expression*
(7)   *expression* ::= [*expression* { + | - }] *term*
(8)   *term*::= [*term* { * | / }] *factor*
(9)   *factor* ::= [*factor* ∕] *primary*
(10) *primary* ::= *number* | *variable* | *function__reference* | *(expression)*
(11) *left__side* ::= *variable*

Fig. 2.1   Simplified extract from ALGOL 60 syntax (based on Naur *et al.* (1963)).

2.2 Variations of the Backus-Naur-form

Alternatives often mean simply that individual constituents are optional:
(4)   *statement* ::= *unlabelled__statement* | *label:*
      unlabelled__statement
This means that a statement may occur either labelled or unlabelled.

Optional constituents and recursive symbols frequently lead to additional non-terminal symbols, which does nothing to assist the legibility of a formal language definition. For this reason, many newer language definitions use the following abbreviations:
(a) Optional symbols or symbol strings are enclosed in square brackets.
(b) Symbols or symbol strings which may be repeated any number of times (including zero repetitions, i.e. the empty string) are enclosed in braces and followed by a superscript asterisk.‡
(c) If the empty string is not included then a superscript plus sign is placed after the braces.

---

† The non-terminal symbols are also known as metalanguage variables in this case.
‡ The asterisk improves legibility, but is not always included (Ichbiah *et al.,* 1979).

12

(d) A part common to all alternatives in a rule is unbracketed; the remaining alternatives are enclosed in braces.

Using this arrangement, the syntax of a programming language can often be described in a more compact and lucid way than with the original method based on the BNF. Fig. 2.1 gives an example of an extract from ALGOL 60.

The observant reader will certainly have noticed that there is a distinct possibility of confusion between terminal symbols and the fixed metalanguage ones:‡ if the separation symbol between alternatives, or the definition sign also occurs as a terminal symbol, then the rules can no longer be unambiguously interpreted. Naur *et al.* (1960) avoided this problem by choosing symbols not occurring in ALGOL 60. If the additional agreements are also included, then neither square brackets nor braces should occur in the language. The problem is essentially removed by underlining the confusion-prone terminal symbols in the language definition:

(5) *subscripted_variable :: = identifier [index {, index} *]*

This method was used in the definition of PL/I (DIN 66255)† and PEARL (DIN 66253).

Finally, we would just mention that the original form of the BNF enclosed non-terminal symbols in angle brackets, thus making the underlined character unnecessary.

One more variant, which can be referred to as the van Wijngaarden form, should be described by way of conclusion to this section. This variant avoids confusion between special metalanguage symbols and terminal ones by also introducing metalanguage symbols for terminal symbols. These differ from the non-terminal ones by adding the word *symbol*. In addition, this definition form, which was devised by van Wijngaarden *et al.* (1969, 1975) for a much more powerful definition method than the one required here, uses the semicolon as the separating sign between alternatives, the colon as the definition sign, the comma for concatenation, and the full stop as the rule end.§

2.3 Syntax diagrams

A formal definition is required in order to avoid misunderstandings, but the concept can be better clarified by means of a graphic representation in the form of a syntax diagram. The following rule will be considered as an example:

(6) *identifier :: = letter { letter | digit } **

This means that an identifier begins with a letter and then as many letters and digits as required can follow on. It can be represented as follows:

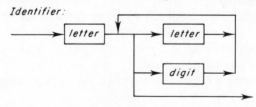

Identifier:

---

‡ Non-terminal symbols can be chosen at will and therefore are more likely to cause less confusion.
† DIN 66255 corresponds to ISO 6160.
§ With normal BNF variations, the end of a rule is found simply by careful scrutiny.

The individual boxes mean that symbols (or symbol strings) of the specified type must be used when arriving at a box along an arrowed line. In the diagram, the first box reached is that labelled *letter*. From there the line can follow any of three alternative directions: another letter may follow, or a digit, or the diagram defining the identifier may be abandoned. In the first two cases, the line returns to the initial branch point.

Fig. 2.2 shows the syntax diagram for rules (1) − (5) in Fig. 2.1. Round boxes are used to denote terminal symbols and square ones for non-terminal symbols.

One further comment must be made in connection with recursion. The box labelled 'block' cannot be simply omitted and the arrowed line returned to the start (before *BEGIN*) otherwise the *BEGIN* symbols would no longer be in agreement with the *END* ones. However, formal language theory shows that recursion can be replaced by a cycle if the recursive symbol occurs at the beginning, or at the end, of a rule. (In our case it is within the body of the rule.)

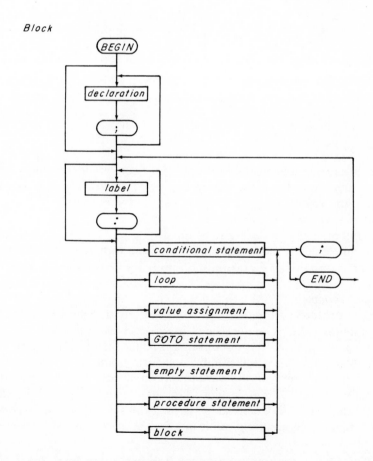

Fig. 2.2   Syntax diagram for rules (1)−(5) in Fig. 2.1.

2.4 Derivation tree

Whereas the syntax diagram represents the syntax of a whole language, the derivation tree represents the structure of an individual fixed program or program section. This tree reflects the substitution steps which can be used to derive specific strings from a non-terminal symbol by applying the rules. The forks in the tree mean that a non-terminal symbol is made up of several constituents, each of which corresponds to one of the branches. The rule

    expression :: = *expression* + *term*

is considered by way of example. This can be represented as follows:

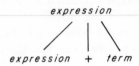

In the same way, one of the possible alternatives for the notion *term* can now be chosen and appended to the tree:†

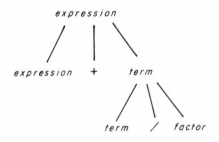

This process of selecting possible alternatives for non-terminal symbols and adding the sub-tree to the main section can be continued. Fig. 2.3 shows the derivation tree representing the structure of the expressions:

    variable − *variable* + *number/variable*

(These symbols could be further substituted.)

This example clearly shows that the Backus-Naur form is in a position to give a correct reproduction of the operator priority. The derivation tree reveals that the section

    number/variable

is the right operand of the plus sign and hence division must be carried out before addition. This is demonstrated by the fact that this symbol string is represented by a sub-tree, the root of which is on the same level as the plus sign.

In the BNF rules, this is achieved by introducing various non-terminal symbols for the operators of the various priority levels to determine which operators may occur in a derivation starting with this symbol. Whereas all operators can appear in a derivation starting with the symbol *expression*, the plus and minus signs are not possible in a derivation starting with the symbol

---

† In contrast to the tree concept used in mathematics, the order of the branches is a significant factor in the derivation tree.

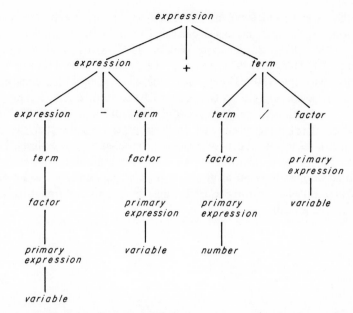

Fig. 2.3   Section from an ALGOL 60 derivation tree. (The 'tails' which appear after multiple substitution of one terminal symbol by another are readily omitted.)

term. (This may be checked using rules (7) – (9) in Fig. 2.1.) Only by using the rule

   primary :: = (expression)

do all operators become possible once more, but this time only in parentheses; this corresponds to the requirement that operator priority can be broken with the help of parentheses.

   The execution sequence from left to right when operators of equal rank meet can also be expressed by the BNF: the left operand of an addition operator, for example, is assigned an expression which can contain addition and subtraction operators as well, whereas the right operand must be a term in which these operators may occur only in brackets.

2.5 Chomsky grammar

At the same time as ALGOL 60 was developed using the BNF as a basis, the linguist Chomsky (1956, 1959) devised a theoretical syntax model, nowadays known as Chomsky grammar, which is close to a formal description of natural language.

A Chomsky grammar is a quadruple $G = (T, N, P, S)$, where T and N represent finite sets of symbols (terminal and non-terminal), $S \in N$ represents a special non-terminal symbol (start symbol), and $P \subset V^* \times V^*$ is a set of productions ($V = T \cup N$).†

V^* is the set of all symbol strings which can be formed from the elements of V.

---

† Based on the assumption that T and N are disjoint.

This theoretical model will not be discussed in any depth: many detailed descriptions of formal languages can be found in the literature (Aho and Ullman, 1972, 1973; Becker and Walter, 1977; Gross and Lentin, 1971; Harrison, 1978; Herschel, 1974; Salomaa, 1973) and its only relevance here is in association with the BNF. The productions $p = (u,v)$, which consist of two symbol strings, correspond to BNF rules of the form $u ::= v$. Hence, each Chomsky production corresponds to only one alternative in a BNF rule. If several alternatives are to be allowed, for example $u ::= v \mid w$, then two productions (u,v) and (u,w) must be incorporated into the set of productions. The BNF does not have the same flexibility as the Chomsky grammar: whereas a Chomsky production may have an arbitrary symbol string on the left side, only one symbol is permitted according to BNF rules. In Chomsky terms, this is known as context-free grammar.

3

Examples

After having indicated the large number of programming languages and the differences between them several times, some examples are essential in order to clarify the points made. Not all languages, and indeed not all the typical constructions of the languages selected, can be covered by the scope of this book. The main emphasis at this point is on a few languages which have had a special influence on language history, and some particular aspects in which they differ. Other aspects and languages will be discussed in subsequent chapters.

3.1 Algol, Fortran

At an early stage, many different research units (Backus, 1978) recognized that programming expenditure on techno-scientific problems could be reduced by adding arithmetic formulae to assembler languages. As Backus reported, this was also the starting point for FORTRAN†. FORTRAN contained arithmetic expressions, Boolean ones added at a later date, plus loops and further language constructions which corresponded directly to machine possibilities, e.g. branches, parameter passing by address reference, and data areas common to several procedures. Hence, the production of an efficient machine program was even then near at hand. However, the language was not standardized until ten years after the first compiler had appeared (FORTRAN 66). This delay led to a number of different implementations. The standard was revised in 1976 – 8 and is now known by the names FORTRAN 77 and FORTRAN V (DIN 66027).‡ Apart from the different implementations, which make it difficult to transfer from one computer system to another, the main disadvantages of FORTRAN are that the identifiers are restricted in length, extensive programs

---

† **Formula Translation**
‡ DIN 66027 corresponds to ISO 1539

18

```
C          Subroutine for determining the greatest value
C          in every line of a matrix
C
           SUBROUTINE linemx(matrix,lineno,clmnno,max)
           DIMENSION matrix(lineno,clmnno),max(lineno)
           REAL matrix,max,partmx
           INTEGER lineno,clmnno,line,column
C
           DO 19   line = 1, lineno
                   partmx = matrix (line,1)
                   DO 17 column = 2, clmnno
                           IF (partmx .GE. matrix(line,column)) GOTO 17
C                          the new value is greater than the others
                           partmx = matrix(line,column)
17                 CONTINUE
19                 max(line) = partmx
           END
```

Fig. 3.1   Example of FORTRAN.

cannot be structured, and word symbols are neither reserved nor especially marked, also spaces may be inserted everywhere within a FORTRAN statement and do not act as a separating character. Fig. 3.1 gives a short example of a FORTRAN program.† FORTRAN programs consist of a main program and an arbitrary number of subroutines, the definitions of which are alongside each other on one level. The outward appearance of the program is determined by the format of punch cards, comment cards must be labelled as such in the first column, labels are in the first five columns and colums 7 – 72 contain declarations and executable statements. Statements are contained on one card unless the following card is labelled as a continuation card by the presence of a digit in column 6.

There is an almost inconceivable number of books about FORTRAN. The literature references here are restricted to some textbooks which give an introduction to the reader who is familiar with a different language (Brauch, 1979; Chirlian, 1973; Gritsch and Gritsch, 1972; Kaucher et al., 1978; McCracken, 1967; Schneider and Jurksch, 1970; Siebert, 1974; Spiess and Rheingans, 1977).

In contrast to FORTRAN, the language definition of ALGOL 60‡ was published before the first implementation (Naur et al., 1960) and thus the language was preserved from any implementation differences (apart from some structures which are extremely complicated to implement, e.g. value arrays). Characteristic features of ALGOL 60 are the hierarchical arrangement of ranges for freely-chosen identifiers (block structure), the possibility of local procedure declarations, and a somewhat more redundant notation. Fig. 3.2 shows the ALGOL 60 version of the algorithm previously formulated in FORTRAN. The outward appearance is determined by the free format and the

---

† In all examples, word symbols which are typical of the language are indicated in capital letters, those that can be selected arbitrarily have small letters.

‡ **Algorithmic Language**

```
COMMENT subroutine for determining the greatest
         value in every line of a matrix;

PROCEDURE linemaxima(matrix,linenumber, columnnumber,maxima);
         REAL ARRAY matrix,maxima;
         INTEGER linenumber,columnnumber;
BEGIN   REAL partialmaximum;
         INTEGER line,column;

         FOR line := 1 STEP 1 UNTIL linenumber DO
         BEGIN partialmaximum := matrix[line, 1];
                FOR    column := 2 STEP 1 UNTIL columnnumber DO
                       IF partialmaximum < matrix[line,column]
                       THEN partialmaximum := matrix[line,column];
                maxima[line] := partialmaximum
         END
END line maxima;
```

Fig. 3.2   Example of ALGOL 60.

specially marked word symbols: neither the line change nor the spaces have any syntactical significance. The word symbols in the language definition, i.e. as defined by the ALGOL report are in bolder print or alternatively they are often underlined. As neither notation can be fed into a computer, DIN 66026† specifies that the word symbols are put in quotation marks. However, some compilers accept a notation with no special labelling.‡

The early and strictly formal definition which has only been very slightly revised (Naur *et al.*, *1963*) has led to implementations which are essentially compatible. However, two very important disadvantages exist which prevent the language being used beyond university level. Firstly, the authors failed to include input and output instructions as a standard language component, although there was a proposal to do so during the definition phase (see retrospective comments (Naur, 1978)). This restricted the possibility of program transferability to the algorithmic core. Secondly, the emphasis lay on the elegant problem oriented formularization of algorithms rather than on efficiency. This led to some language structures which were certainly flexible, but did not allow any efficient machine program to be generated (e.g. call by name for parameters).

Many books have also been written about ALGOL and again only a few of these are named here (Alefeld *et al.*, 1972; Anderson, 1964; Dijkstra, 1962; Guntsch and Schneider, 1972; Herschel, 1976; McCracken, 1962; Schauer, 1977; Schneider and Jurksch, 1970).

3.2 Cobol

The need for problem-oriented programming languages for commercial and administrative purposes became apparent very early on. However, unlike

---

† DIN 66026 corresponds to ISO 1538 which is withdrawn.
‡ See footnote † on p. 18 for our notation.

```
IDENTIFICATION DIVISION.
PROGRAM-ID. CALCULATION.
ENVIRONMENT DIVISION.
CONFIGURATION SECTION.

    ...
INPUT-OUTPUT SECTION.
FILE-CONTROL.
            SELECT purchase-cards ASSIGN TO card-reader.
            SELECT invoice ASSIGN TO printer.
DATA DIVISION.
FILE SECTION.
FD purchase-cards
            LABEL RECORD OMITTED
            DATA RECORD IS purchase.
Ø1          purchase.
            Ø2 article-no          PICTURE IS 9(6).
            Ø2 description          PICTURE IS X(2Ø).
            Ø2 individual-price     PICTURE IS ZZ9.99.
            Ø2 quantity             PICTURE IS Z9.
FD          invoice
            LABEL RECORD OMITTED
            DATA RECORD IS invoice-line.
Ø1          invoice-line            PICTURE IS X(54).
WORKING-STORAGE SECTION.
Ø1          line.
            Ø2 quantity             PICTURE IS Z9.
            Ø2 FILLER               PICTURE IS XX.
            Ø2 article-no           PICTURE IS 9(6).
            Ø2 FILLER               PICTURE IS XXX.
            Ø2 description          PICTURE IS X(2Ø).
            Ø2 individual-price     PICTURE IS ZZ9.99.
            Ø2 FILLER               PICTURE IS XXXX.
            Ø2 price                PICTURE IS Z(4)9.99.
Ø1          final-line.
            Ø2 FILLER               PICTURE IS X(43).
            Ø2 sum                  PICTURE IS Z(4)9.99.
```

Fig. 3.3a   Example of COBOL (declaration section).

efforts made in the techno-scientific field, most of the interest was centred on one language alone: COBOL.§ The first language definition was drawn up and published in 1959 – 60. However, later developments were based on COBOL 61 which was not completely compatible with the initial one. COBOL 65 was used as the basis for a later standard (DIN 66028).† As with FORTRAN, COBOL showed that programming languages are living languages with the advantage of adaptability on the one hand, and the disadvantage of having different versions

---

§ Common business oriented language
† DIN 66028 corresponds to ISO 1989.

```
PROCEDURE DIVISION.
start.
        OPEN INPUT purchase-cards
             OUTPUT invoice.
        MOVE ZEROES TO sum.
next-article.
        READ purchase-cards RECORD AT END GO TO end.
        MOVE CORRESPONDING purchase TO line.
        MULTIPLY individual-price OF line BY quantity OF line GIVING price.
        ADD price TO sum.
        WRITE invoice FROM line.
        GO TO next-article.
end.
        WRITE invoice FROM final-line.
        CLOSE purchase-cards, invoice.
        STOP RUN.
```

Fig. 3.3b   Example of COBOL (algorithm).

on the other. In contrast to FORTRAN with its many subsets which are incompatible with each other, COBOL has the advantage of being upwards compatible to a large extent.

The outward appearance of COBOL programs (Fig. 3.3) is characterized by a good deal of verbalization, and most of the statements are formulated in English. Hence, sentences begin with a verb and end with a full stop. The main principle is to use as few verbs as possible (i.e. statement types) and ensure expressibility by using a number of options within the sentences. As Sammet (1978b) observed retrospectively, the first priority was to give the language a natural design. This was also the reason for giving the program a hierarchical structure, dividing it up into divisions, sections and paragraphs. Each program consists of four divisions: the *IDENTIFICATION DIVISION* describes the program and author, the *ENVIRONMENT DIVISION* refers to the peripheral equipment, the *DATA DIVISION* gives details of the data structure, and the *PROCEDURE DIVISION* describes the algorithm. Column position is an important factor: division, section, and paragraph headings begin in column 8, and the statements begin in column 12.

Two essential differences between this and the techno-scientific languages must be mentioned. On the one hand, COBOL allows hierarchically-structured data structures, in which both individual components and whole or part structures can be used as operation objects; on the other hand, it contains no flexible procedure concept.

Again, the literature section contains only a small selection of all reference works published on COBOL (Armstrong, 1973; Geissler and Geissler, 1974; McCracken, 1978; Mickel, 1975; Murach, 1978; Singer, 1972).

3.3 Successors

The first generation languages triggered off a spate of further developments, from which just four have been singled out here: (1) PL/I, which was an attempt to create a language that would be equally suitable for any application area; (2) BASIC, which is a minimum language in the sense that all computable functions can be described using as few language elements as possible; (3) ALGOL 68, the most significant aspect of which is the way that the syntax and semantics of programming languages have been most thoroughly investigated; (4) PASCAL, which represents a new era in the history of programming languages combining elegant formulation, efficient translation, and better use of running time.

As Radin (1978) reports, PL/I† emerged from research into further development of FORTRAN. An initial version was published by Radin and Rogoway (1965) (still under the name NPL). As already mentioned, the thinking behind it was to create a system for solving all types of problems. So, not only did PL/I take the algorithm structuring in the form of loops, alternatives, and flexible procedures from ALGOL, but also the hierarchical data structuring, and the various input and output alternatives from COBOL as well. In addition, it contains language structures for creating and synchronizing concurrent processes which feature in system implementation and real time programming. This variability of application range results in variability of requirements, which in turn involve a number of different language constructs incorporating a certain number of exceptions. Hence, PL/I comprises the static storage management of FORTRAN, management depending on the block structure of ALGOL, and management controlled by the programmer. Another example lies in the fragmentation facility of the block structure for declarations. Consideration of all the programming language concepts represented by PL/I goes beyond the scope of this book. Our presentation is based on the language parts described in the literature (Katzan, 1972; Lecht, 1968; Rechenberg, 1974; Schulz, 1975, 1976).

BASIC‡ is the exact opposite of PL/I. The language was devised by Kurtz and Kemeny in 1963 – 4. Kurtz (1978) explained later that the idea evolved from the problem of giving non-technical students, who nevertheless needed some knowledge about data processing, an insight into the problems of programming. This resulted in a small number of language constructs (only 14 originally) incorporated into a special 'operating system' involving simple commands and based on the English language.

The most obvious feature of the outward appearance of BASIC programs (Fig. 3.4) is the line numbering. This facilitates editing in the interactive mode; the programmer needs to enter only one new program line in order to change, extend, or delete the original one. Another salient feature is the very short identifiers which are even shorter than the FORTRAN ones. The language, therefore, is more suitable for a rapidly written program, visible at a glance, than for a long-term one involving a good deal of maintenance.

In contrast to languages referred to so far, BASIC does not have any declarations and must, nevertheless, be regarded as a mode-bound language, as the form of the identifier determines the object mode.

---

† Programming language I
‡ Beginners all-purpose symbolic instruction code

```
100   SUB linemx(m(,),n1,n2,x())
104   REMARK Subroutine to determine greatest value
105   REMARK in any line of a matrix.
110   FOR z = 1 to n1
121       LET    v = m(z,1)
131       FOR    s = 2 TO n2
142              IF v > = m(z,s) THEN 162
152              LET v = m(z,s)
162              NEXT s
171       LET    x(z) = v
181       NEXT z
190   SUBEND
```

Fig. 3.4   Example of BASIC.

The limited language scope of BASIC makes it suitable not only for those unfamiliar with computer science, but it was also ideal for the first microprocessor-based desk computers which have made a significant contribution to its popularity. At the present time, more BASIC systems are on offer than any other. The same applies to programming guides, of which just a few are mentioned here (Albrecht *et al.*, 1973; Haase and Stucky, 1977; Kemeny and Kurtz, 1970; Menzel, 1980; Schärf, 1975; Spencer, 1974).

ALGOL 60 was the starting point for many language developments. According to Pratt (1975), ALGOL 68 is the most important one to emerge. He is certainly correct as regards the theoretical foundation of the subject and the systematic language design, but its popularity does not rate so highly. The language emerged from the IFIP[†] working group involved in further developments of ALGOL 60. The definition was published by van Wijngaarden *et al.* (1969) and they later produced a revised report (van Wijngaarden *et al.*, 1975); the concept is described by van der Meulen and Kühling (1974, 1977).

The outward appearance of an ALGOL 68 program (Fig. 3.5) is similar to that of an ALGOL 60 one. At first glance, the only obvious features are the consistent application of the bracket principle and a certain functionality. The well-known principle of surrounding a sequence of units by opening and closing brackets is transferred to all language structures: each language structure begins with an opening bracket symbol and ends with the corresponding closing one. This means that nesting can be done arbitrarily without having to consider special cases. ALGOL 68 is functional, in the sense that each language structure has a function value which can be further processed by a surrounding structure.[‡] When investigated more thoroughly, it is clear that, like BASIC, ALGOL 68 makes do with a smaller number of concepts, but obtains a greater degree of expressibility, due to the fact that these concepts can be combined almost arbitrarily (orthogonality). This flexibility makes the language easier to deal with, once it is known, but makes the learning process more difficult.

---

† International Federation of Information Processing Societies.
‡ A few structures, e.g. branch instructions, lead to an undefined function value.

```
PROCEDURE linemaxima = ([,] REAL matrix) [] REAL:
BEGIN [1:1 UPB matrix] REAL partialmaximum:†
        REF REAL pointeronpartialmaximum;
        FOR line FROM 1 BY 1 TO 1 UPB matrix
        DO pointeronpartialmaximum
            := partialmaximum[line] := matrix[line,1];
            FOR column FROM 2 BY 1 TO 2 UPB matrix
            DO IF pointeronpartialmaximum < matrix[line,column]
                THEN (REF REAL : pointeronpartialmaximum)
                    := matrix[line,column]
                FI
            OD
    OD;
    partialmaximum
END
```

Fig. 3.5   Example of ALGOL 68.

Lindsey and van der Meulen (1971) refer to it as follows: 'Since ALGOL 68 is a highly recursively structured language, it is quite impossible to describe it until it has been described.'

Of all the languages stemming from ALGOL 60, PASCAL has achieved the greatest acclaim. Wirth (1971) founded the language on both a didactic and technical basis. The didactic aspects are the same as those for BASIC: few fundamental concepts, clear natural structure, and simple syntax. However, it takes into account the aspect of systematic programming which was very widely discussed during the GOTO controversy‡. The language was supposed to contribute to program reliability and give insight into the organization of somewhat larger software projects. Finally, Wirth proved that problem-oriented programming languages also give efficient target programs, and in addition this could be achieved by a rapid and simply structured compiler. These objectives were achieved firstly by adopting the structure of expressions and statements from ALGOL 60. Then came structured data giving the possibility of programmers defining data modes themselves and identifying them by a problem-oriented symbolic name. Finally, a large number of control structures were incorporated. However, the fact that the readily readable compiler was written in PASCAL itself and was more or less freely available, and that it could be adapted for other systems at very little cost was a major factor in its widespread acceptance. A short example of a PASCAL program is given in Fig. 3.6.

The great popularity of PASCAL has of course meant the publication of many books (Herschel and Pieper, 1979; Hosseus *et al.*, 1980; Ottman and Widmayer, 1980; Schauer, 1979, 1980). Two books, however, deserve special mention: one is important because of the examples it gives (Bowles, 1977) and the other includes a definition of the language (Jensen and Wirth, 1978).

---

† *n UPB a* determines the *n*th upper bound of array *a*.
‡ See ch. 10.

```
PROCEDURE linemaxima(matrix: realmatrix;
                        linenumber,columnnumber: integer;
                        VAR: maxima: realvector);
VAR line, column: integer;
    partialmaximum: real;
BEGIN
FOR line := 1 TO linenumber DO
BEGIN  partialmaximum := matrix[line, 1];
        FOR column := 2 TO columnnumber DO
            IF partialmaximum < matrix[line, column]
            THEN partialmaximum := matrix[line, column];
        maxima[line] := partialmaximum
END;
END
```

The procedure requires the global declarations

TYPE realmatrix = ARRAY[1:linenumber, 1:columnnumber] OF real;
TYPE realvector = ARRAY[1:linenumber] OF real;

Fig. 3.6   Example of PASCAL.

3.4 Special trends

A problem-oriented programming language should be based on the method of writing or speaking commonly used in the field of application for which it is intended. So, it is hardly surprising to find that some programming languages are very different in both internal and external structure from ALGOL, FORTRAN, COBOL and their successors. We mention three of these languages: APL, LISP and SNOBOL.

APL† was devised and published in the early sixties by Iverson (1962). As Falkoff and Iverson (1978) explained at a later date, the objective was to produce a tool with which various computer science themes could be described and analysed, and which could be used for instruction and for writing books. The language has an amazingly simple syntax which possesses only three forms of statement, no operator priority, and only functions with zero, one or two parameters. The effect of operators is defined irrespective of whether the parameters are scalars, vectors or matrices; extending operator effects from scalar to structured objects always happens in accordance with the same scheme. Apart from this, compound operations are possible as Fig. 3.7 shows. As a result of these high level operators, APL can work with a very elementary flow control. This does not give rise to obscurities as long as the only problems considered are those which manipulate matrices and similar objects. Falkoff *et al.* (1964) published a very impressive example showing how APL was suitable for describing hardware facts, even before the first APL implementation appeared.

The small number of basic concepts has played a decisive role in establishing the popularity of APL as a dialogue language. When a programming language is used in conversational mode, it is important that the programmer can keep the rules in his head and does not have to keep looking through papers. At first

---

† A programming language

a) With the /-operator: (pmx = partialmaximum)
   ∇ *dummy* ← *linemax matrix*
 [*1*] *dummy* ← *//*[*2*] *matrix*
   ∇

b) Without the /-operator:
   ∇ *dummy* ← *linemax matrix*
 [*1*] *line* ← *1*
 [*2*] *pmx* ← *matrix*[*line; column* ←*1*]
 [*3*] → *5* × ι *((ρ matrix)* [*2*] < *column*← *column* + *1)*
 [*4*] → *3, pmx* ← *pmx* ⌐ *matrix*[*line; column*]
 [*5*] *dummy*[*line*] ← *pmx*
 [*6*] → *2* × *(ρ matrix)* [*1*] ⩾ *line* ← *line* + *1*

Fig. 3.7 Example of APL.

glance, the large number of operators seems to contradict this, but Giloi (1977) gave the following explanation: the fact is that APL objects are ordered sets and the operators must be associated with known set operations (Grey, 1973; LePage, 1978).

In contrast to all the languages described so far, any discussion of LISP† presents problems. There are a number of dialects which do not have merely insignificant differences. The concept started with the work done by McCarthy during the period 1956 – 62; at the end of this period LISP 1.5 was implemented (McCarthy *et al.*, 1962). This version fathered a number of dialects such as MACLISP, INTERLISP, RLISP, MLISP, CLISP, etc. LISP was developed for application in artificial intelligence which had no long term history of established terminology presupposing an agreement on the model concepts behind it. Further developments in this field thus led to various language dialects and indeed to various languages too (Rieger *et al.* (1979) give a review of recent developments). Marti *et al.* (1979) have recently defined a common subset in the light of experience obtained in the meantime; Deransart (1979) has put forward a way in which the various dialects could be based on such a standard concept.

LISP differs from the other programming languages considered so far, in that its objects are symbolic expressions which can only be executed by special instructions (Fig. 3.8). In particular, program parts can be considered as data in their turn and be modified. The functional style of writing and recursion are two further characteristics. The functional style means that all operations whether they be standard or user defined appear as functions with parameters. Apart from this alternative, recursion is the only means of influencing control flow. The small number of constructs means that a LISP interpreter can be recorded essentially on one page (McCarthy, 1978). An introduction to LISP is also given by Allen (1978) and Stoyan (1978).

In the age of text processing, SNOBOL‡ and its highly developed symbol string operations cannot be omitted from this survey. The language was

---

† **List** processing
‡ **String** oriented symbolic language

Symbolic differentiation of a LISP expression
(LABEL differentiate
  (LAMBDA (f x)
    (COND ((ATOM f)(COND ((EQ f x) 1)
                          (T   Ø)
)   )
      ((EQ (CAR f)(QUOTE PLUS)) LIST ((QUOTE PLUS)
                                       differentiate ((CADR f) x)
                                       differentiate ((CADDR f) x)
)   )
      ((EQ (CAR f)(QUOTE TIMES))
            LIST ((QUOTE PLUS)
                  LIST ((QUOTE TIMES)
                        (CADDR f)
                        differentiate ((CADR f) x)
)
                  LIST ((QUOTE TIMES)
                        (CADR f)
                        differentiate ((CADDR f) x)
)))   )   )

Fig. 3.8   Example of LISP.

developed in various stages from 1962 onwards by Lee, Griswold (1978), Polonsky and Farber. From the beginning, it was designed for use in automatic text processing. The operations on and with character strings are especially characteristic of this: concatenation, searches for given character strings to be part of a larger one, replacement and deletion of part strings. The concept of a pattern was introduced in an attempt to give increased flexibility to these processes; this takes the form of a search tree which can be freely defined by the user and with which the character string can then be compared (the successful branch can be established by means of variables ascribed to the pattern). Tables were then introduced, the elements of which can be addressed by their contents in a similar manner to the associative memory. All these concepts are dynamic

start	*character = LEN(1) . new*	
	letter = 'ABCDEFGHIJKLMNOPQRSTUVWXYZ'	
	number = TABLE(700)	
	old = ' '	
input	*OUTPUT = INPUT*	*: F(RETURN)*
	text = OUTPUT	
nextchar	*text character =*	*: F(input)*
	letter new	*: S(count) F(nextchar)*
count	*number <old new> = number <old new> + 1*	
	old = new	*: (nextchar)*

The procedure must be declared by *DEFINE('countletterpairs',* *'start')*.

Fig. 3.9   Example of SNOBOL.

and require a long runtime. In total contrast to the highly structured objects and powerful operators, there are the very elementary control structures which do not include any advanced structures for alternatives or loops; even a procedure body has to be skipped by branch instructions; Griswold *et al.* (1976) give a detailed introduction and an example is shown in Fig. 3.9.

4

Objects and object modes

4.1 Object modes

Each algorithm describes a sequence of more or less elementary operations which are applied to given data. Obviously, it would not make sense to apply all computer operations to all data. This is a known mathematical fact and hence mathematical propositions generally begin with a formulation such as

let a, $b \in R$ with $a \geqslant 0 \ldots$

let $(G, +)$ be a commutative group ...

let $f: M \to N$ be a function ...

This tells the reader what properties the object has, what possible combinations there are with other objects, and what relations can be tested between this and other objects. An object set does not acquire any practical significance until operations and relations have been defined, for it is these possibilities which allow us to work with the objects:

Object mode or type implies a number of objects together with a set of operations and relations.†

Each programming language contains some standard object modes. In general, the integer numbers, numerically real numbers, logical values, alphabetic characters, and the character strings formed from this alphabet are all included.

The numerically real numbers will be considered as the first example of an object mode. The underlying object set (range of values) is a computer-dependent finite subset of mathematically real numbers. This is a result of the finite word length of the computer and is therefore responsible for the fact that operations using numerically real numbers agree only approximately with those using real ones. Dyadic operations which are defined on the numerically real

---

† Strictly, objects which play a special role (such as 0 or 1) should also be incorporated. However, they may be regarded as the result of parameterless operations.

numbers are addition, subtraction, multiplication, division, and exponentiation (the latter applies especially for techno-scientifically oriented languages). Monadic operations are identity and negation. (Although both can almost always be characterized by the signs for addition and subtraction, the two are intrinsically different.) Operations such as square root, logarithms, etc. could be included with the monadic group but most programming languages ascribe them, from a notational point of view, to the functions because they are composed of elementary operations (e.g. APL considers the natural logarithm as a monadic operation). The order relations ($<$, $\leqslant$, $=$, $\geqslant$, $>$, $\neq$) are dyadic relations. Comparisons with the constant 0 could basically be regarded as monadic relations (positive, non-negative, etc.), but this is not normally the case. One example of a monadic relation can be found in the object mode of integers: testing if the operand is even or odd.

Most programming languages use the infix style in which the operator is placed between the two operands. This excludes operations with three or more parameters which can only be expressed as functions. One exception is LISP which uses the prefix style and thus incorporates operations and relations with an arbitrary number of operands in uniform notation (see chapter 6).

The mode of lists which consist of objects of a given basic mode, e.g. integers, is considered by way of a second example. Those lists in which new elements are added only at one end and entered elements removed only from the other (queues) are considered here.

The following five operations, given here in mathematical notation with the definition range on the left and the range of values on the right of the arrow, are of interest for the purpose of working with such queues.

create:		$\rightarrow$	*queue*
add:	*queue* $\times$ *elements*	$\rightarrow$	*queue*
first:	*queue*	$\rightarrow$	*elements*
remove:	*queue*	$\rightarrow$	*queue*
empty:	*queue*	$\rightarrow$	$\{$ *true, false* $\}$ †

The example shows that useful applications are possible by not restricting the operands and results to elements of the considered object mode. In addition to the queue set, the properties of which are relevant in this instance, the set of elements from which the queue is made up and the set of logical values are also present.‡

The programmer often has to work with problem-specific objects which are not in the programming language because the wide range of possibilities forbids it. One such example is represented by the days of the week. In the classical programming languages, the programmer had to encode such objects by representing them by integers. Hence program legibility has benefited from the possibility which the more recent programming languages have to offer of defining an object mode by enumerating its elements (enumeration mode). Obviously, no operations and relations other than equality and inequality tests are defined in

---

† For those readers not familiar with mathematical notation, 'add' is dyadic; the first operand and the result are queues, the second operand is from the set of elements.
‡ Mathematics refers to this as a heterogeneous algebra.

this way. However, if element enumeration is interpreted implicitly as an order (and PASCAL is an example of this (Jensen and Wirth, 1978)), then the monadic operations *predecessor* and *successor* and the order relations $<$, $\leqslant$, $>$, $\geqslant$ become meaningful.

4.2 Type conversions

In the case where an operator symbol can be meaningfully applied to various object sets, it characterizes various operations. The operator symbol $+$ may be considered as an example: when applied to the set of integers, it means the addition of integers giving an exact result, and it is generally carried out inside the machine by fixed point addition; when applied to the set of numerically real numbers, it represents floating point addition which can only be performed approximately; and finally, it is used in some programming languages to indicate concatenation on the set of character strings.

This multiple application of operator symbols does not result in obscure programs provided that one object mode can be mapped into the other so that both operations coincide. This is then called a mode extension. B is a mode extension of A if there is a function $f: OB_A \rightarrow OB_B$ which attributes to each object of set A an object of set B† and satisfies a compatibility condition between operations and relations respectively: if op_A is a dyadic operation defined in A, then there is a dyadic operation op_B in B, and f, $(A_1\ op_A\ A_2) = f(A_1)\ op_B f(A_2)$ holds. Hence it does not matter whether the operation is performed in A and the result is then transformed to B or whether both operands are transformed and then the operation is carried out in B. Suitable compatibility conditions would also be imposed for non-dyadic operations and for relations. Use of the same operator symbol is justified in view of the consistent effects of the two operations.

The standard example for mode extension is the mapping of integers into numerically real numbers as provided by almost all programming languages (FORTRAN 66 is an exception). If x is numerically real and i and j are integers, then the compatibility condition makes it immaterial whether the statement $x: = i + j$ is performed in the range of integer numbers and the result converted to the real value range, ‡ or whether i and j have already been converted and then a real value addition is carried out.

It may be argued that, in the case of embedding the integers into the real ones, the compatibility condition does not apply for division. For this reason, many programming languages use different symbols for the two forms of division. Nevertheless, embedding can still take place, because division can be based on the other operations both in the integer and real value range. Hence, to demand the compatibility conditions for those operations and relations which are elementary for the considered object mode is sufficient.

---

† In practice, mainly injective functions arise but this is not compulsory: it is easy to imagine that the object mode 'date' is embedded in the object mode 'weekday' in such a way that the operation *next__day* satisfies the condition.

‡ The word 'numerically' will be omitted from now on.

In contrast to mode extension, ALGOL 60 involves the mode contraction of real numbers onto integers in which the former are rounded. If x and y are real and i is an integer, then different results are obtained for the statement $i := x + y$, depending upon whether the addition is performed before or after the transformation from reals to integers. (This can be illustrated by using the values $x = 3.8$ and $y = 4.9$.) With this type of mode conversion, special attention must be paid to the sequence of operations.

A safe mode contraction, from a program methodology point of view, is offered by the submodes available in the more recently developed languages. Finally, we would like to refer to the subtle concept of ALGOL 68 which offers a large number of mode conversions, the application of which is dependent on operand context.[†]

4.3 Type declarations

Each programming language has a set of standard object modes. The more recent languages also offer the facility for the programmer to enter additional problem oriented object modes. Four stages can be distinguished:

(1) The object set can be established without operations other than the equality and inequality test being defined. This does not exclude additional operations from being separately defined. ALGOL 68 can be regarded as an example of this.

(2a) For the enumerated modes, the enumeration of the elements can be said to imply an order and the order relations $<$, $\leqslant$, $>$, $\geqslant$, and the operations *SUCCESSOR, PREDECESSOR, FIRST* and *LAST* are automatically defined. PASCAL can be used as an example, despite the fact that *FIRST* and *LAST* are not included.

(2b) The object set is established as a subset of objects of an already existing mode and all operations defined there are accepted on the condition that the result is still in the subset. The *subrange type* of PASCAL is an example.

(3) The object set is defined together with arbitrary, problem oriented operations. The oldest examples of this are SIMULA 67 (Nygaard and Dahl, 1978) and CLU (Liskov *et al.*, 1977).

(4) The language provides the opportunity to formulate a mechanism describing how new types of objects are composed from others, and how operations on the former are based on those defined on the existing modes. Former modes do not need to be specified at the time of definition; the new mode is parametrized. CLU is an example of this.

Cases (3) and (4) belong to the data modules for which Goos and Kastens (1978) have drawn up a classification.

As widely-used programming languages allow no mode declarations—with the exception of PASCAL and even that can only cope with stages (1) and

---

† This is given in tabular form by Lindsey and van der Meulen (1971, p. 208)

(1)   *TYPE matrix IS ARRAY (integer, integer) OF real;*
       TYPE date IS
              RECORD   day: integer RANGE 1..31;
                      month: integer RANGE 1..12;
                      year: integer RANGE 1900..2000;
            END RECORD;
       TYPE tick IS DELTA 1/60 RANGE 0..3600;
(2a)   *TYPE colour IS (white, red, yellow, green, blue, brown, black);*
(2b)   *SUBTYPE small_number IS integer RANGE - 127..127;*
       SUBTYPE rainbow IS colour RANGE red..blue;
       SUBTYPE second IS tick DELTA 1;
(3)   *PACKAGE rational_ numbers IS*
              TYPE rational IS
                    RECORD counter: integer;
                            denominator: integer: RANGE 1..integer;
                            LAST;
                  END RECORD;
                  FUNCTION " = " (X, Y: rational) RETURN boolean;
                  FUNCTION " + " (X, Y: rational) RETURN rational;
                  ...

    END
(4)   *GENERIC*
              TYPE element_type IS PRIVATE;
              size: integer;
       PACKAGE queue IS
              queue_range: ARRAY (1..size) OF element_type;
              PROCEDURE add (element: element_type);
              FUNCTION first RETURN element_type;
              ...

    END

Fig. 4.1   Object type declaration in ADA.

(2)—examples from ADA will be considered.† Fig. 4.1 shows first of all the declaration of three object modes with no operations defined on them. Objects in the mode *date* each consist of three components which are integers with some conditions imposed. Objects in the mode *tick* are multiples of 1/60 occurring in the range 0 to 3600. As an order is implicitly defined for the enumerated modes in example (2a), an interval from *red* to *blue* can be assumed, and then used in a subtype declaration *rainbow*; the subtype inherits the order. In the same way, the subtype *small_number* takes on the arithmetic operations defined on the integers as long as they do not go beyond the specified range. Example (3) defines the type rational numbers as a set of integer pairs together with their corresponding operations (in this case, the denominator must be positive). The induced equality relation would then regard two rational numbers as equal only if both components are identical, but this does not conform with the usual con-

---

† For some time, a standard language definition was only available as a report by the American Department of Defence. This definition deviated in some places from Ichbiah *et al.* (1979). Some English textbooks are now available (Pyle, 1981).

cept of equality $(4/6 = 2/3)$, so that the equality test for rational numbers must be newly defined in addition to arithmetic operations. The final example shows how a queue is obtained for an element type including those not yet defined. If a concrete element type and a dimension are substituted in using this *generic* declaration, then the corresponding object type will be generated. The construction of arbitrary array types (*array*) is a special case within this concept and is generally available in programming languages.

One final explanatory note is in order at this point: the notions mode and type are not standardized in literature and as a result, there is very little difference between them. In this book, they are used synonymously.

4.4 Programming language objects

So far, objects have appeared only as an abstract concept. They must be identified before they can be used in programs.

A programming language object is defined to be a pair made up of an identifier and an internal object:† *plo = (id, iobj).*

The internal object can only be picked up via its identifier. The relation between identifier and internal object is unambiguous with respect to the latter; thus a unique internal object is assigned to each identifier. Conversely, the same internal object can belong to several identifiers: for example, the identifiers *7* and *007* have the same integer as internal object (according to the interpretation of common programming languages). Moreover, the relation between identifier and internal object remains unchanged within a definition range (see chapter 8).

The syntax of each programming language defines which identifiers are allowed or prescribed for programming language objects. There are standard and arbitrarily chosen identifiers. Standard identifiers are provided in any programming language for constant objects of the available standard modes, e.g. integers, real numbers, character strings, etc. Arbitrary identifiers are needed so that the programmer can label objects which he himself has entered. In all the more recent programming languages, identifiers can also be used to identify known standard constants in order to improve the legibility and maintainability of the program.

A variable is often understood to be an identifier to which different values can successfully be assigned during a program run. This formulation is neither flexible nor accurate enough to cover more than the classical, simple, and indexed variables. Programming language objects, as defined above, comprise passive objects (data), and active objects such as procedures, coroutines, or processes in which the internal object is a rule for computing a numerical value. Thus, the concept of a variable must be based on that of the programming language object.

---

† Bauer and Goos (1971) use the notion value here, but this almost always has a different meaning in books on programming languages.

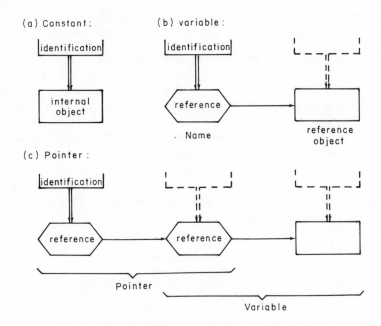

Fig. 4.2   Constant, variable, and pointer.

A variable consists of a pair of programming language objects in which the internal object of the first component (name) is a reference to the second component (referenced object).†

Behind this definition is the machine-based concept that an address is the internal object corresponding to the indentification of a name and the reference is produced by feeding the referenced object into the storage cell thus addressed. Lindsey and van der Meulen (1971) use the diagram shown in Fig. 4.2 for a clear interpretation of the programming language object, as do Bauer and Goos (1971). Fig. 4.2b shows clearly that identification of the referenced object is of no relevance: its internal object can be reached via the identification of its name. However, it is plain that this same identification also permits access to the reference. The syntax and semantics of a programming language must establish which of these two internal objects is meant when the identification appears in a program.

As the referenced object can, for its part, contain a reference to a further object, the result is a whole hierarchy of objects with different reference levels:

A constant (object 0. reference level) is a programming language object, the internal object of which has no reference to another object. A name (object 1. reference level) is a programming language object whose internal object is a reference to a constant. A

---

† The referenced object in the variable is generally given as the value of the variable in books on programming languages. The procedure example reveals the following problem: the referenced object is a rule for computing a numerical value, whereas the intuitive understanding of procedure value is the result of its execution.

pointer (object $(i + 1)$th reference level) is a programming language object whose internal object is a reference to an object of the ith reference level ($i \geq 1$).

The pointer can also be interpreted automatically in a machine oriented way: its internal object can be understood as the address of a storage location whose content is the address of the referenced object. Fig. 4.2c shows clearly the context in which pointers can be used effectively; the internal object refers to the name of a variable, but the identification of this name does not necessarily have to be known in the program. Thus, pointers are used in the first instance if a previously undefined number of new variables have been created during the program run. The fact that the number of these is unknown does restrict the choice of suitable identifiers when the program is drawn up. Secondly, pointers may be used in conjunction with composite objects with a view to preventing a repeated evaluation of access paths.†

4.5 Value assignments

The concept of variables is meaningful only if it is linked with the possibility of assigning various referenced objects.

A value assignment is defined to be a statement which creates a reference between a name and a referenced object. Access to the referenced object of a variable always gives the object which was assigned last in the dynamic program run.

Until the first value assignment, the referenced object of a variable is undefined, i.e. various translators can provide different specifications. Only a very few languages incorporate initialization into their definition; for example, SNOBOL initializes all variables with the empty character string.‡ FORTRAN and COBOL and most of the newer languages offer the programmer the possibility of assigning a referenced object to a variable at the time of its creation (see section 5.4).

Value assignments occur in programs both explicitly and implicitly. Certain aspects of parameter processing in subprograms belong to the second group, and input statements plus those statements which are usually identified in the narrowest sense as value assignments or assignment statements fall into the first category. Only the form in which they are written and the possibility of assigning a new referenced object to several variables, if necessary, differ from one language to the next. Fig. 4.3 shows the different forms. In general, a variable identifier is on the left side of a value assignment.§ (The variable identifier may be expressed more accurately as the identification of the name of a variable.) The referenced object to be assigned is on the right side, and this can be given in three ways (1) by its identification, (2) by the identifier of a variable to which it has been assigned previously, and (3) by a rule for computing a numerical

---

† The program examples in the ALGOL 68 report use this concept at several points (van Wijngaarden *et al.*, 1969)
‡ Many FORTRAN translators effect the initialization of all variables with 0. As this does not correspond to the language definition, the programmer should not rely on it.
§ The exception is the COBOL statement MOVE where the sequence is changed.

language	single	multiple
ALGOL and successors	$a := e$	$a := b := e$
PASCAL	$a := e$	
FORTRAN	$a = e$	
- for label variables	$ASSIGN\ m\ TO\ a$	
PL/I	$a = e$	$a, b = e$
SNOBOL	$a = e$	
LISP	$(SETQ\ a\ e)$	
BASIC	$LET\ a = e$	$LET\ a, b = e$
APL	$a \leftarrow e$	$a \leftarrow b \leftarrow e$
COBOL	$MOVE\ b\ TO\ a$	
- only for arithmetic	$COMPUTE\ a = e$	
- for field subscripts	$SET\ a\ TO\ c$	$SET\ a, b\ TO\ c$

Fig. 4.3   Value assignment form (a, b = identification of variables; c = identification of variables, or constants; e = identification of variables, constants, or a rule for computing a numerical value to determine an object; m = identification of a label).

value, evaluation of which gives the future referenced object. Cases (2) and (3) may require mode conversion. Whereas case (3) requires evaluation of the numerical value computing rule (deproceduring), the transfer of the name of a variable to its referenced object (dereferencing) is sufficient in case (2). Figs. 4.4a and 4.4b show this process for objects of the first and second reference levels.

Value assignments are required for working with variables. This applies for all object modes irrespective of whether it is a standard type or one defined by the programmer. A glance at the classical programming languages shows that this requirement was not always generally valid. Neither ALGOL 60 nor FORTRAN (up to FORTRAN 66) allow value assignments for compound modes; in ALGOL 60 there is not even an explicit value assignment for the character string standard mode.

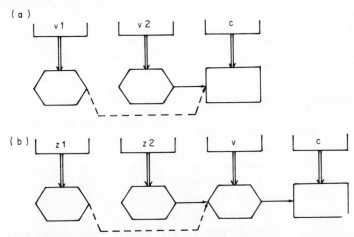

Fig. 4.4   Value assignment after dereferencing (a) at variable level, (b) at pointer level. The dotted lines are formed by the value assignment.

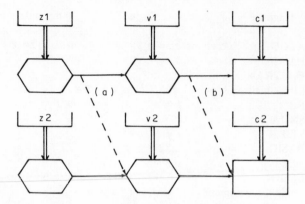

Fig. 4.5 If the two pointers z1 and z2 take part in a value assignment, the language definition must establish when the value assignment proceeds in accordance with (a), and when it follows (b).

| | value assignment at the level of: | |
	(a) pointer	(b) variables
ALGOL 68	$z1 := z2$	$mode\ (z1) := z2$
	$z1 := v2$	$mode\ (z1) := v2$
PASCAL	$z1 := z2$	$z1\uparrow := v2$
	$z1 := v2$	$z1\uparrow := z2\uparrow$
BLISS	$z1 := .z2$	$.z1 := .v2$
	$z1 := v2$	$.z1 := ..z2$
SIMULA	$z1 :- z2$	$z1 := z2$
	$z1 :- v2$	$z1 := v2$
ADA	$z1 := z2$	$z1.ALL := z2.ALL$
	$z1 := v2$	$z1.ALL := v2$
PL/I	$z1 = z2$	$vz1 = vz2$
	$z1 = ADDR(v2)$	$vz1 = v2$

Fig. 4.6 Value assignment notation at pointer or variable level. $z1$, $z2$ are declared as pointers, $v2$ as a variable, $vz1$ and $vz2$ as in a BASED declaration. (In PL/I, $z1 \rightarrow v1$ may be required instead of $z1$ and $vz1$.)

If the identifier of a pointer is on the left side of a value assignment, then it is not clear initially which reference arrow should be altered (Fig. 4.5). This represents a special case of a more general problem: wherever the identifier of a pointer occurs in a program, this can represent (1) the name of the pointer, (2) the name of the referenced variable, and (3) the constant most recently assigned to the variable. Hence, it must be made clear whether dereferencing is to be carried out (a) not at all, (b) once, or (c) twice. As the identification context often clarifies which is the case, a wide variation of regulations is possible (Fig. 4.6). ALGOL 68 contains a very detailed set of rules which specify which mode conversion is possible in which context (Lindsey and van der Meulen, 1971; van Wijngaarden *et al.*, 1969): for a value assignment, dereferencing takes place on the right side until a reference level below that on the left is attained; it is done on the left side if the resultant mode is given. BLISS adopts the opposite position, in which each dereferencing level must be given and labelled with a dot placed in front of the identifier (Wulf *et al.*, 1971). PASCAL characterizes dereferencing by an arrow placed after it, and implicitly assumes a dereferencing step on the right side of the value assignment (Jensen and Wirth, 1978). SIMULA solves the problem with various assignment symbols (Dahl and Nygaard, 1968).†

---

† Apart from technical reports, there does not seem to be any summary reviews of SIMULA 67 in existence. The various papers published by Dahl and coworkers (Dahl, 1968; Dahl and Nygaard, 1968; Dahl and Hoare, 1972) are taken as a basis.

5

Declarations

The definition of any programming language establishes certain standard identifications which are available to the programmer. He can also select others arbitrarily, but in most cases he must make statements about the properties in a special declaration section.

A new programming language object is created by an identity declaration; this assigns an arbitrarily chosen identification to an internal object. The internal object may be introduced either (a) by a standard or previously defined identification, or (b) implicitly. The former leads to several identifications being ascribed to the same internal object, and is especially important for programming methodology. The second case is important for the declaration of first- and higher-level reference names, where the internal object corresponds to the address of a storage location or area.

A mode declaration introduces a new object mode by establishing objects and the permitted operations associated with them. Thus, the more recent programming languages incorporating this mechanism give the programmer the opportunity of introducing those object modes which are suited to the problem in question.

Finally, module declarations give control over the validity, access, and existence range of objects and declarations; these aspects are discussed in chapter 8. Mode declarations were covered in section 4.3 and labels, procedures, and exception conditions, which are identity declarations but are also relevant to control flow, are described from chapter 9 onwards.

5.1 Significance of declarations

Internal objects are represented by bit strings in computer systems. Programmers and compilers require a description of how the bit string is to be interpreted in order to work with these objects. This description is necessary because its mode is not obvious from the bit string alone. The object mode is fixed by a declaration. There are some programming languages which prescribe an invariable mode for each object and some which do without this altogether (type-free languages). If the mode is specified, this can occur explicitly or implicitly.

Examples of type-free languages are APL, LISP and SNOBOL.† However, they work very well with fixed object modes. Type freedom simply means that the mode is not explicitly declared, and objects of various types can be assigned to the name of a variable successively as referenced objects. This transfers the control of correct object use from the compiler to the programmer. A declaration is important to the reader of a program because the essential properties of the individual objects and the permitted operations are contained in the program text. Although these are known when writing the program, they certainly must be known when the program is maintained. Type-freedom counters the requirement, which is generally accepted today, that programs should be reliable and easily checked at translation time.

However, declarations are also meant to give the compiler information on the objects used. The object mode gives information about the size and structuring of the storage area needed by the individual object, the acceptability of operator symbols, and the implementation of operations.

Size and structuring of the storage area required by the various objects can differ greatly. Hence, both logical values can be represented by a binary digit, integer or real numbers are usually represented by one or more words, and composite objects generally require more space. Not every operator symbol makes sense irrespective of the range of values; for example, the operator symbol + is only used for arithmetic operands. The translator can only check these restrictions if the declarations are implicitly or explicitly available to it. The realization of operations is often dependent on the type of operand: inside the machine, addition of integers is usually implemented by fixed-point addition and that of real numbers by floating-point addition. The exact type of operand must be known in order that the correct operation is applied. (This problem also relates to union modes, structures with variable format, and generic functions.)

Declarations are also important for the efficiency of the program created and of the program construction process. The latter profits not only from the documentation value but also from the possibility of improved error recognition and diagnosis by the compiler. The efficiency of the program created depends in many ways on the knowledge of a complete object description. Thus, for example, knowledge of object structure can be used to achieve as efficient storage as possible; in the case of composite objects, the reading and writing access to the individual components can be optimized.

Finally, information in the declaration, and the position of the declaration in the program can indicate the lifespan of the object, i.e. creation and deletion points (see chapter 8).

---

† In this sense, SETL is type-free and BLISS is partly so (Dewar *et al.*, 1979; Wulf *et al.*, 1971).

5.2 Identity declarations

Identity declarations can occur explicitly and implicitly. Explicit ones are preferable to implicit ones since they give better program reliability and documentation. Whereas explicit declarations may be scattered arbitrarily in FORTRAN 66 programs, most languages specify a comprehensive declaration division (*DATA DIVISION* in COBOL) at the beginning of the corresponding range. Labels are generally only declared at that point of the program which they identify.† An explicit declaration is made up of the identification of the object being declared and its mode specification. With constant declarations, the object value is also incorporated, and with initializing ones, the initial referenced object is included.

Implicit declarations are based on the premise that the object mode is given by the form of identification or by the context in which the object occurs. BASIC and FORTRAN are examples of the former and PL/I the latter. In FORTRAN, identifiers with the initial letters *I, J, K, L, M, N* identify integer objects and all others identify real objects unless the programmer has made an explicit declaration to specify otherwise. (The *IMPLICIT* declaration in FORTRAN 77 means that another set of rules for initial letters can be drawn up.) One example for context declaration in PL/I is the implicit identification of a file from its appearance in an *OPEN* statement. Implicit declarations do not correspond to the demands for reliable programs for various reasons: first of all, they can only be used as a general rule for pre-defined standard modes and secondly they prevent error detection. In this context, it is remarkable that despite being a type-free language BLISS demands the explicit declaration of all objects (Wulf *et al.*, 1971).

Declarations for objects of the first reference level in the ALGOL language family and FORTRAN are not very different (Fig. 5.1). In the basic form, identifiers, of which several may be specified in a list, follow the mode option; only the array declarations place the size associated with the mode‡ after the identifier, thus splitting up the mode specification. FORTRAN further splits up declarations by allowing the element mode and the fact that an array is involved to be specified in different declarations. PASCAL has a format which makes it explicitly clear that the name of the variable is involved. BLISS has no mode-bound objects and hence no mode specifications. However, it does require a storage specification in order to establish the data control form (see chapter 8). For example, the specification REGISTER means that this identifier identifies a register. In its strict language form, ALGOL 68 uses a formulation which reflects the graphic description shown in Fig. 4.4. The right side of the declaration contains the description of the internal object, whereas the left side establishes the mode. The difference between the 'formal' and 'actual' declarer is not shown by the simple variables, but can be seen from the array declaration:

$$REF\ [,]\ REAL\ r = LOC\ [1:10,\ 1:10]\ REAL\S$$

---

† PASCAL, which also requires a pre-declaration in this case, is an exception.
‡ The size specification implicitly defines the number of indices belonging to the mode description, whereas the size itself usually does not.
§ *LOC* refers to the storage administration.

ALGOL 60	*mode identifier*
	mode identifier [*size— specification*]
FORTRAN	*MODE identifier*
	element— mode identifier (size— specification)
	DIMENSION identifier (size— specification)
PASCAL	*VAR identifier: mode*
ADA	*identifier: mode*
BLISS	*storage— specification identifier*
	storage— specification identifier [*size-specification*]
ALGOL 68	*REF formal— declarer identifier*
	= storage— specification actual— declarer
PL/I	*DECLARE identifier attribute— list*
COBOL	*level— number identifier PICTURE IS format.*

Fig. 5.1   Object declarations (first reference level).

The right side means that the internal object must refer to an object which consists of 100 real quantities (a shortened notation is available, as this method of writing is very awkward).

5.3 Special cases: PL/I and COBOL

In PL/I identity declarations, the object mode is fixed by a combination of various attributes. For example, five attribute groups are available for numeric objects and these can be combined in any way at all: (1) it may involve an array with given subscript bounds; (2) there may be a choice between storage in the binary or decimal system; (3) in storage, the quantity may be represented as fixed point or floating point; (4) objects can be restricted to real values or complex values can be accepted; (5) accuracy can be prescribed by establishing precision; for fixed point numbers, the number of places after the point must be given in addition to the total number of digits. The following is an example:

DECLARE   x BINARY FIXED REAL (15,0),
y DECIMAL FIXED REAL (10,2),
z BINARY FIXED COMPLEX (15,0),
a(1:20) BINARY FLOAT REAL (15),
u(1:10) BINARY FIXED REAL (15,0).

There are two ways of reducing the amount of writing involved: by using implicit pre-specifications, and factorization. There are pre-specifications for all attribute groups and these are always used when the programmer has not provided a specification in that group. However, these pre-specifications are dependent on the other attributes; hence, for example, *DECIMAL FIXED* has an implied accuracy of *(5,0)*, but in contrast *DECIMAL FLOAT* has an implied accuracy of *(6)*. Factorization means that the common components can be

44

unbracketed and this means a shorter method of writing for concordant attributes.†

DECLARE ((x,u(1:10)) REAL,
z COMPLEX) BINARY FIXED (15,0).

The concept of building up object modes at this level by combining various attributes is very flexible on the one hand, but leads to complicated mode conversions on the other.

As is the case with most languages which allow explicit declarations, the identity declarations of COBOL are placed in front of the algorithm in a special declaration section known as the *DATA DIVISION*. Here there is a difference between the declaration of input/output data (*FILE SECTION*) and that of other data (*WORKING-STORAGE SECTION*). As COBOL is designed for applications which involve a lot of input/output operations, object declaration places less value on the object mode in the algorithmic sense than on the external representation of data. Hence these declarations contain specifications which are reserved for the input/output statements in other languages (Fig. 5.1). The format may include up to 30 characters which can be numerical positions represented by *9*, alphabetical positions (*A*), alphanumerical positions (*X*), position of an assumed decimal point (*V*), and sign (*S*). Whilst these characters are also used for the declaration of intermediate results, the zero suppression (Z), insertion of blank spaces (B), and explicit positions for decimal point (.) and sign (− or +) are only required for the declaration of I/O objects.

As structured objects play an important part in COBOL applications, all objects are declared by the level numbers used to define structured objects (chapter 7). The level number 77 is given to simple non-composite objects.

5.4 Initialized declarations

Provided that the declared object is not a constant, many programming languages can expand the declaration by incorporating initialization. Otherwise, the referenced object of the variable is undefined up to the first explicit value assignment, i.e. a different value can be in force for each implementation. (Hence, a warning should be given against the widely used practice of taking advantage of an implicit initialization available in a special implementation unless prescribed by the language definition.)

The point in time at which initialization takes place depends on the type of storage administration used as a basis (chapter 8). Clarity is important in the case of dynamic storage administration because the storage area for the referenced object is available only during the lifetime of the variable. Thus, initialization cannot take place until the program run reaches this range and it must be repeated for each new entry. With static storage administration, it is often accepted that initialization takes place at the start of the program. However, this is only consistent if the declaration is universally valid. Local

---

† When subsequent changes are made in a developed program (maintenance) this facility becomes somewhat questionable.

variables result in inconsistencies, as the draft standard for FORTRAN 77 shows: on the one hand, it specifies that initialization takes place at the start of the program, and on the other, that local variables lose their defined value when leaving the validity range so that initialization takes effect only when the first call, e.g. of a subroutine, is made. As this deviates somewhat from the meaning of initialization, a special ruling is required for local variables which occur in a *DATA* declaration (for further details see *Draft proposed ANSI FORTRAN (1976)*).

ALGOL 68	*declaration : = expression*
ADA	*declaration : = expression*
PL/I	*declaration INITIAL constant*
COBOL	*declaration VALUE IS constant*
FORTRAN	*declaration*
	DATA identifier/constant/
SNOBOL	*implicit initialization*

Fig. 5.2   Initializing declarations.

Fig. 5.2 shows that initialization is almost always achieved by adding a suitable clause to the actual declaration. Only FORTRAN separates initialization from declaration. In SNOBOL, any declaration is linked to an implicit initialization creating a reference to the empty string.

When involved with the initializing declaration of compound objects, the programmer needs to know whether he must write a constant explicitly for each component or can abbreviate multiple occurrence of the same constants. FORTRAN and PL/I use the following iteration factor for this purpose.

DATA field_identification/50*0.0, 10*1.0/
ADA refers to indices, selectors or ranges:
  field: ARRAY (1..60) OF real : = (1..50 = > 0.0, OTHERS = > 1.0)

In general, initialization must be done with constants. Initialization involving an expression is only meaningful if its evaluation is deferred until its range is reached at run-time.†

5.5 Declaration of constants

A constant is a programming language object, the internal object of which is not a reference to another object. Hence, the aim of constant declaration is to assign an arbitrarily selectable and thus problem related identifier to an object entered in a different way. Labels and procedures are examples of this type of constant object in all programming languages. The internal object of a label is a program position; declaration takes place at the relevant program position itself. The internal object of a procedure is a computation rule.

The classical languages such as ALGOL 60, COBOL and FORTRAN 66 contained no constant declarations, but the value of documentation was subse-

---

† So-called 'compile time' expressions are constants.

ALGOL 68	*mode identifier = expression*
PASCAL	*CONST identifier = constant*†
ELAN	*mode CONST identifier :: expression*
ADA	*identifier; CONSTANT mode : = expression*
FORTRAN 77	*PARAMETER identifier = constant*

Fig. 5.3   Constant declarations.

quently recognized and this facility was incorporated into later versions. The notations are very different (see Fig. 5.3). ADA supplements the initializing declaration solely by the symbol *CONSTANT*; ALGOL 68 makes the difference clear by using the equality instead of the value assignment symbol. PASCAL and FORTRAN 77 do not indicate object mode; it is implicitly determined by the right side. However, this restricts constant declaration to standard object modes. Unless the mode is specified, obscurities arise when used in conjunction with self-defined object modes. For example, if the mode *dayofthemonth* is introduced as a sub-type of *integer*, then the mode of a constant declared with the right side *15* is not clear because this standard identification identifies a constant in both modes.

The concept of constant definition involves more than standard mode constants, for which the programming languages offer standard identifications, and constants entered by identity declarations. The 'compile-time constants', the identification of which has the syntactical form of an expression, also belong to this category. If this concept is encountered in programming handbooks, it is usually approached in one of two different ways: (1) Identification of a rule for computing a numerical value; it is at a position where arbitrary expressions are permitted, and is evaluated only at translation time on optimization grounds. This aspect of compile-time constants is possible in any programming language. (2) Identification of a constant which is itself unknown at the point at which the program is formulated, but for which the rule for calculating it from other constants is known. At the position where there must actually be a constant, the programmer inserts the rule for computing a numerical value; this is evaluated at translation time and thus gives the required constant. This aspect obviously allows expressions at all the positions where constants must exist. It has met with success in more recent times and is also considered in FORTRAN 77.

In ADA, ALGOL 68 or ELAN (Hommel *et al.*, 1979), for example, the internal object does not have to be capable of determination at translation time. The fact that it is present when the program run enters the declaration range is sufficient. This has the advantage of allowing the identifier to identify another constant at each run through the range. The increased efficiency of a program which can be achieved by this was recognized very early on in connection with procedures (*VALUE* concept in ALGOL 60).

More recent discussions on programming languages have concluded that the property of an object to be a constant or to be the name of a higher reference level is not inseparably bound up with the object. When setting up reliable soft-

---

† *CONST* appears in front of the first constant declaration only.

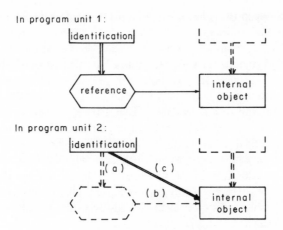

In program unit 1:

In program unit 2:

Fig. 5.4   Reduction in access rights.

ware, it is often better that the value assignments to change a variable are restricted to one program unit, whereas the other program units are allowed to read it only. The object is regarded syntactically as a constant there. The read-only attribute of EUCLID enables such a construction (Lamport *et al.*, 1977).†
In Fig. 5.4, the object in program unit 2 behaves as if the double arrow (c) exists instead of arrows (a) and (b). (This would also be covered by an ALGOL-68 constant declaration with a variable identification from program unit 2 on the right side.) However, EUCLID permits an intermediate change in reference arrow (b) by calling up a procedure declared in program unit 1 and allows (c) to take part in this change. The arrow (c) should therefore be regarded as a shorter version of access paths (a) and (b).

On the pointer level, there are even more possibilities due to the larger number of arrows which are discussed, for example, by Ichbiah *et al.* (1979). BLISS already provides the facility of linking complex access paths with recently declared identifications (Wulf *et al.*, 1971).

5.6 Identifiers

Declarations serve to assign an arbitrarily selected identification to the objects used in the program. A specification for these identifiers has been drawn up and very few languages actually deviate from it.

An identifier is made up of as long a string of letters and numbers as necessary, beginning with a letter and separated by the insertion of interruption characters.

The strictest length impositions are found in COBOL (30 symbols), FORTRAN (6 symbols), and BASIC (3 symbols). However, there are a whole series of languages in which identifiers of any length may occur in the program text, but which use only an implementation-dependent leading part of specified length to

---

† BALG (Goos, 1976) is another example of this type of language.

differentiate between two identifiers. SNOBOL is an example of a language in which the whole of an identifier is significant, whatever its length.

Long identifiers are an advantage for the documentation value of the program text. Visual structuring is often required in this case on legibility grounds. The following interruption symbols are used: blank space (ALGOL,† FORTRAN), underlined blank space (PL/I, ADA, SNOBOL), minus sign (COBOL) and the full stop (SNOBOL). EUCLID entrusts the determination to each implementation, and also permits a switch from small to capital letters.

Languages vary as to whether the interruption signs are of any syntactical importance. (1) It may be a sign like any other, in which case a new identifier is created by its introduction (PL/I, COBOL, SNOBOL, ADA). (2) It may be of no significance for differentiation purposes (ALGOL, FORTRAN). (3) It may be that no identifiers differing only in interruption signs are allowed in the same range (EUCLID).

Some special forms are also available. BASIC only allows a letter which can be followed by a digit for identification of arithmetic variable names. Arithmetic valued arrays are identified solely by a letter. Identifications for string variables and corresponding arrays consist of a letter followed by a dollar sign. For standard functions, three letters are used; for programmer-defined ones, identifiers acceptable to the result mode preceded by *FN* are used. This regulation is so detailed because it contains the declarations implicitly. COBOL also allows identifiers which begin with a number, as long as they contain at least one letter. Some languages allow certain special characters to be used as 'letters': $, @, # in PL/I; in APL: Δ and underlined letters; in BASIC: $, ρ, # (note that all these are older languages).

---

† Only possible in implementations in which word symbols are specially characterized.

6

Standard object modes

In modern programming languages, the following object modes are standard: integers, logical values, alphabetic characters. This list is supplemented by numeric-real numbers of single and double precision, and complex numbers for languages with a techno-scientific bias, and by character strings for those oriented towards non-numerical problems. As already mentioned in section 5.1, these object modes also exist in the so-called type-free languages.

Then there are standard mechanisms with which compound objects can be formed from simple ones. Again, differences based on the language application field are apparent: the techno-scientifically oriented ones allowed arrays from the beginning and commercial-administrative ones involved records. Other compound forms play a part in artificial intelligence (linked lists, sets) or text processing (character string patterns). In some languages, character strings are not considered as independent object modes but as an array of individual symbols.

6.1 Arithmetic operations

In problem oriented programming languages,† for pragmatic reasons, the arithmetic object modes are not so sharply distinguished as that provided by the clear-cut definition of the object mode concept. Hence, these modes are considered collectively.

Numbers in problem oriented programming languages are generally represented in the decimal system: a decimal number is a sequence of an arbitrary number of decimal digits, in which a decimal point separates the whole from the fractional part, and which can be followed by an exponent part.

---

† Machine oriented languages differentiate more accurately and use different instructions for integers or real numbers.

Integers are regarded as those numbers which contain neither a point nor an exponent part. All others are known as real numbers. FORTRAN accepts that a number ends with a decimal point whereas other languages such as ALGOL and COBOL do not. Complex numbers are represented as a bracketed pair of real value quantities; in some languages, integers can also be considered as components of complex numbers (e.g. PL/I).

Operations allowed on the arithmetic modes are: arithmetic operations, relational operations, and type conversions between the individual arithmetic modes. The four basic methods of calculation, addition, subtraction, multiplication and division together with exponentiation in some languages, are available as binary arithmetic operations. Identity (unary plus) and negation (unary minus) represent unary arithmetic operations. Out of the six possible relational operations, only equality and inequality are of any importance for complex operands. Type conversions may be explicit or implicit; the implicit type conversions are required for so-called mixed-mode expressions in which integers, real, and complex quantities can occur simultaneously.

As regards the notation of binary operations, there are two common forms, the normal infix notation

operand operator operand

and the prefix notation

operator operand operand

which is used infrequently in the basic arithmetic modes but is used more frequently in other operations. In LISP, prefix notation† is found also with the fundamental arithmetic modes, e.g. *(PLUS 1 3)*. In all other operations, this notation is much more common and indeed is the only one to apply for operations having more than two operands:

MOD (4,3)   MIN (7, −3, 6)

Most programming languages accept infix notation only for operations previously defined in the language and the programmer must use prefix notation (functions) for self-defined operations.

Addition and subtraction are uniformly represented by the operation symbols + and − which can also be used for the unary operations of identity and negation (apart from APL). Multiplication is generally represented by an asterisk (∗). Only ALGOL 60 and APL provide a special multiplication sign (×). Whereas the unusual abundance of the APL character set generally requires a special keyboard, most ALGOL-60 implementations use an asterisk in its place (DIN 66006).

The problem with division is that it is a restricted operation in the integer range. ALGOL 60 and languages derived from it therefore distinguish between whole number division ($\div$, '/', //), which requires two integer operands and gives an integer result and division defined on real value operands (/). As a result of the implicit mode extension (from INTEGER to REAL) this can also be used for integer operands. FORTRAN identifies both forms of division by the same symbol: *4/3 = 1* but *4.0/3.0 = 1.333...*

---

† Prefix notation has the advantage of requiring no special priority rules (chapter 9).

The ALGOL 60 Report defines that exponentiation gives an integer result if and only if the base is an integer and the exponent is a non-negative integer. Thus, the mode of intermediate results cannot be checked at translation time. Hence, implementation with a real value result is normally the rule. In FORTRAN, integer operands give an integer result which is 0 with negative exponents (conforming to the rules for division). Exponentiation is shown by ∕ in ALGOL 60 (language definition) and BASIC, * in APL, and **, which is also a substitute version of the arrow, everywhere else.

6.2 Special features of arithmetic operations

Almost all programming languages use the same characters to denote the signs for identity and negation. In fact this causes no problems because, as far as the result is concerned, it does not matter whether the symbol represents a sign or a unary operation. When unary and binary operations come into contact, brackets or removal from a sub-expression can be used to make things clearer (*3∗(− 4)* or *− 3∗4*). Problems only arise if the programming language allows such a contact for systematic reasons: (1) ALGOL 68 gives the unary operations priority over the binary ones (*3∗ − 4* corresponds to *3∗(− 4)*) and uses no signs in the program, preferring to regard them as unary operations. (2) SNOBOL places unary operations directly in front of the operands, whereas binary ones are separated from both operands by a space. (3) APL also gives priority to unary operations and distinguishes the negative sign from unary negation and binary subtraction by putting it at a high level (*3 × ⁻4* that is *3 × − 4*).

COBOL presents a different form of notation for arithmetic operations. The difference between this and other programming languages is in the verbal identification of operations and the destruction of the second operand:

ADD operand1 TO operand2
SUBTRACT operand1 FROM operand2
MULTIPLY operand1 BY operand2
DIVIDE operand1 INTO operand2

In each case, the referenced object (instantaneous value) of the second operand is replaced by the result of the operation; the operation implies a value assignment. If this value is to be assigned to another variable, then

GIVING variablename

must be added to the statement.† Note that when dividing, the second operand is divided by the first. The arithmetic expressions commonly used in other programming languages can be used in association with the originally unavailable verb *COMPUTE* (see section 4.5).

6.3 Arithmetic constants

A programmer can start with the assumption that the integers occurring in the program are represented exactly. As the possible number range depends on the

---

† In the *ADD* statement, *GIVING* replaces the standard *TO*.

computer, the prescription for an 'arbitrary number of digits' is of a purely theoretical nature, and means only that the language definition contains no specification on the largest possible integer that may be used. So, care must be taken when transferring programs which have relatively large integers to another computer. BASIC provides seven positions for single precision and 15 for double; COBOL provides 18 positions. The more recent languages tend to record the largest number as a distinguished programming language object with its own identification, e.g. ADA, with *integer 'LAST*.†

Only a restricted number of positions can be processed for numeric real numbers. However, for most techno-scientific purposes, the last positions of overlong numbers can usually be disregarded. On the other hand, the size of intermediate and final results is often so dependent on input data that it is an unknown factor at the time the program is written. Hence, programming languages designed for this application range incorporate floating point numbers $z = m.b^e$, whereby only m and e are stored in the computer. The uniqueness required for internal representation can be achieved by the condition $b^{-1} \leqslant m < 1$. With floating point numbers, relative accuracy is given by the position number of the mantissa m and size by the exponent part b^e. The base $b = 10$ is used for program notation quite independently of internal representation.

ALGOL 60 uses the special symbol $_{10}$ as a separating sign between mantissa and exponent and $'$ or E as a substitute representation; in all other cases, E is normally used for single and D for double precision.‡ The precision of floating point numbers depends on the position number used for the mantissa and is therefore machine-dependent. PL/I and ADA allow the programmer to prescribe the required precision together with the declaration of floating point objects. When subtracting numbers which are roughly similar in size, an apparent precision of the result is due to mantissa standardization within the range b^{-1} to 1.

This apparent precision can be avoided by working with fixed point numbers which are multiples of a prescribed increment and lie within a prescribed range (£ amounts or data from measurements are examples). Languages belonging to the ALGOL family and FORTRAN regard only the integers as fixed point numbers (increment 1) and all those with a fractional part as floating point numbers. APL and PL/I classify only numbers with exponent parts as floating point numbers. Disregarding non-standardized extensions, COBOL recognizes only fixed point numbers. Whereas these languages allow only powers of 2 and 10 as increments for fixed point numbers, ADA allows any incrementation at all.

Arithmetic operations can give intermediate or final results which lie outside the specified range or which cannot be represented by the incrementation specified. In some cases (COBOL!) the 'outstanding' positions are cut off without warning; this leads to unreliable programs. To cope with this type of

---

† ADA allows the attribute *LAST* for all scalar modes.

‡ E stands for exponent, D for double precision.

situation, COBOL makes use of the options *ROUNDED* and *ON SIZE ERROR,* ADA has *CONSTRAINT_ERROR* and PL/I *ON OVERFLOW.*

The internal representation of numbers does not depend on the use of the decimal system in the recorded program. The construction of computer systems from elements which are capable of two states implies the use of a binary system. This is only important to the programmer in one special way: a truncated decimal fraction cannot always be represented by a truncated binary fraction but may have to be represented by a recurring one, e.g. $(0.1)_{10} = (0.000110011...)_2$. In techno-scientific applications, this is only of any consequence when very many of these rounding errors are added up. In commercial and administrative fields, the requirement for an exact representation of truncated decimal fractions is of much greater importance and hence COBOL and PL/I incorporate internal representation in the decimal system. In PL/I, this is done by including the attribute *DECIMAL* or *BINARY* in the declaration. COBOL allows only decimal representation, in which the attribute *USAGE IS DISPLAY* requires one byte per decimal position, whereas *USAGE IS COMPUTATIONAL* leads to a packed representation with four bits per decimal position (BCD representation). Some COBOL implementations also allow *USAGE IS COMPUTATIONAL − n* (with $1 \leqslant n \leqslant 9$); the binary fixed point and floating point representations are amongst these non-uniformly used attributes.

6.4 Logical value mode and relations

In most program examples, logical values are the result of relations between integers and real numbers. Notation is varied even in languages using infix notation, (Fig. 6.1). Apart from the operations outlined, COBOL also includes a comparison with zero (*IS POSITIVE, IS NEGATIVE, IS ZERO,* with *NOT* as an option).

ALGOL60 (DIN)	FORTRAN	COBOL	PL/1	PASCAL BASIC	ADA
= *EQUAL*	.EQ.	*EQUAL TO*	=	=	=
≠ *NOT EQUAL*	.NE.	*NOT EQUAL TO*	¬ =	< >	/ =
< *LESS*	.LT.	*LESS THAN*	<	<	<
⩽ *NOT GREATER*	.LE.	*NOT LESS THAN*	< = ¬ >	< =	< =
> *GREATER*	.GT.	*GREATER THAN*	>	>	>
⩾ *NOT LESS*	.GE.	*NOT GREATER THAN*	> = ¬ <	> =	> =

Fig. 6.1 Relational operations. COBOL incorporates the abbreviated = for *EQUAL TO*, > for *GREATER THAN*, and < for *LESS THAN*, and these can all be combined with *NOT*.

A general observation should be made here: the equality and inequality tests are suitable for any object mode and should therefore be defined for any object mode and identified uniformly for all.† This has only been recognized by the

---

† In ALGOL 60 the equality test is not defined for character string mode and is identified for logical value mode by ≡.

more recent languages. When comparing pointers, rules should be drawn up to ascertain if the equality/inequality test should check whether both pointers indicate the same variable (ADA) or whether the same constant is assigned to the referenced variables (ALGOL 68 ‡). SIMULA uses $= =$ and $=/=$ on pointer level and the normal ALGOL 60 operations on variable level.

The other relational operations are useful for any mode which is based on an ordered element set. This applies in particular to alphabetical modes and enumerated modes defined by the programmer himself. In the case of alphabetical modes, either the order should be fixed by the programmer (e.g. ADA) or the 26 letters of the Latin alphabet should occur in their correct sequence and without any gaps.§

If an order is defined for a mode, then it is useful to extend this alphabetical order to all arrays which are made up of components of this type. The type of character string which is made up of individual characters is a special example. Alphabetical order means that one array comes before another if the element in the first of the differently made up components is 'smaller' than the corresponding element in the other array.†

	Usual representation	PL/1	APL	LISP
Negation	*NOT*	¬	~	
Conjunction	*AND*	&	∧	*LOGAND*
Disjunction	*OR*	|	∨	*LOGOR*

Fig. 6.2 Boolean operations.

The result of a relation is expressed by one of the two logical values *TRUE* or *FALSE*. Most programming languages recognize the operations of negation, conjunction, and disjunction (Fig. 6.2), so that all Boolean functions can be formed. BASIC is an exception: it does not recognize these operations and hence relations cannot be combined in conditional statements. Some languages offer additional operations. APL contains the *NAND* and *NOR* operations (⍲ and ⍱) for negating conjunction and disjunction respectively, ALGOL 60 has the implication $(A \wedge B) \vee (\neg A) = \neg A \vee B$ and ADA has the exclusive disjunction *XOR* which appears to be superfluous because it concords with $\neq$. Boolean operations are often used on bit vectors or Boolean vectors component by component, and in this case, *XOR* can be used differently from $\neq \cdot$

One special feature of conjunction and disjunction is that it is not always necessary to evaluate both operands in order to get a result (Huskey and Wattenburg, 1961). For example, if the left operand of a conjunction has the value *FALSE*, then the right one plays no further part. The definition in almost all programming languages omits any specification of whether the second

---

‡ As long as the standard preface is used.
§ Some implementations use computer-dependent internal representations and the order resulting from them.
† In APL, the comparison of arrays is carried out component by component and gives a Boolean array as a result.

operand is to be evaluated in this case. If this is not so, then a condition $I > 0 \wedge A[I] = \ldots$ is processed without any error detection even if $I = 0$ and $A[0]$ is not defined, whereas error does occur when both operands are evaluated. Thus, error detection is dependent on implementation. ADA gives the programmer the possibility of choosing more rapid evaluation by means of *AND THEN* or *OR ELSE*, in association with conditional statements.

6.5 Characters and character strings

The characters of an alphabet are regarded as a special case of the enumerated mode in the more recent languages. The older ones did not offer such a facility. Languages differ with respect to: (1) how the constants of these modes are identified, (2) whether a specific alphabet is prescribed, (3) whether an order is defined on the object set,† and (4) whether type conversions are possible from and into the set of integers. The trend is towards acceptance of the 128 characters of the ASCII-character set, thus giving the order and the mapping onto the interval between 0 and 127. The character strings are formed by concatenating individual characters; they tend to be regarded as character arrays and to be processed accordingly (see chapter 7).

Variables in which the referenced objects are character strings have a varying degree of flexibility in the different programming languages, and this all depends basically on storage administration. (1) In languages with static storage administration such as COBOL and FORTRAN 77, the referenced objects which can be assigned to a name are always of the same length. Hence spaces must be added, or excess characters cut off if necessary, for value assignments. The programmer must make sure that the length rules are adhered to when character strings are concatenated or sub-strings substituted. (2) The declaration fixes a length for the referenced objects which can be assigned to a name, but this is interpreted as an upper limit rather than a strict length. The PL/I declaration, with its *VARYING* attribute, and BASIC, in which the upper limit is always 18, belong in this category. (3) The length of the referenced object can vary arbitrarily as is the case in APL and SNOBOL. This facility, which is very convenient for the programmer, has the disadvantage that the storage area required cannot be determined at translation time and must therefore be acquired at run time.

Increasing use is made of a delimiting symbol rather than brackets for representation of character and character string constants.§ Single quotation marks are used in ADA, APL, BASIC, FORTRAN 77, PASCAL, PL/I and others, and double ones in ADA and COBOL.‡ ADA also permits the percentage sign (%) as an alternative. SNOBOL accepts both forms so that one character can always appear, without special provision, in character strings which are delimited by the other. In the majority of languages, the delimiter

---

† See discussion on relational operations in section 6.4.
§ Fortran 66 uses the representation *nHtext* in which *n* is the number of characters in the text after the *H*. The notation was not adopted by FORTRAN 77.
‡ ADA uses single quotation marks for characters and double for character strings.

character should be doubled when it occurs within the character string, for example,

'GRIMM''S FAIRYTALES' or *''''*

in which the second example represents a character string consisting of one apostrophe only. If a quotation mark is to appear in a COBOL character string, the string has to be split up and the quotation mark inserted by means of its identification *QUOTE:*

"GRIMM", QUOTE, "S FAIRYTALES"

In its language definition, ALGOL 60 uses the different symbols 'and' with substitute representations '('and')' for the beginning and end of a character string. The concept behind this is that character strings can be provided with a nested structure. LISP is another special case, where the character strings are symbolized by the preceding symbol *QUOTE*.

The empty character string can also be represented by delimiting characters, whereby the opening and closing ones follow in direct succession. In SNOBOL, even the delimiting characters can be omitted for the blank character string.

The majority of languages do not distinguish between the individual characters and a one-character string and use the same delimiting signs for both. ADA is the only one which does make the distinction.

6.6 Character string operations

The more recent languages process character strings as arrays of an enumerated mode, so that the same operations apply as they do there.[†] A few observations on some of the older languages, e.g. PL/I, COBOL and SNOBOL in particular, are given below.

Whereas PL/I allows the normal relational operations on characters and character strings and takes the alphabetical order based on the EBCDIC code, COBOL allows relational operations on character strings only as part of the *SORT* statement; the order used depends on the implementation, but it can be assumed that the space character comes before the alphabetic characters which are in turn followed by the numeric ones; the alphabetic and numeric characters are always arranged in their natural sequence. The order in SNOBOL is also dependent on implementation but can be requested by the constant *&ALPHABET.* SNOBOL incorporates the equality test *IDENT (X, Y)*, the inequality test *DIFFER(X, Y)* and the alphabetic greater than symbol *LGT(X, Y)*.

If a language does not process character strings as an array[‡] of individual characters (PL/I) then a type conversion between these two modes is desirable. PL/I offers the standard function *STRING (array_identification)* for converting an array into a character string. One type conversion which is important in text processing problems is the conversion of character strings which identify an arithmetic constant into the corresponding arithmetic mode. SNOBOL permits this conversion implicitly within arithmetic expressions: *PI = '3.14'* and then *X = 5*ZK*. PL/I also has a similar type conversion in which the reverse is also

---

† See sections 4.3 and 6.4, and chapter 7.
‡ EUCLID defines this as a record composed of length and an array.

possible. An inquiry as to whether a character string represents the identification of an arithmetic constant can be made by *INTEGER (character__string)* in SNOBOL and *IS[NOT] NUMERIC* or *IS[NOT] ALPHABETIC* in COBOL.

New character strings can be obtained by concatenation, i.e. the linking of two character strings. Concatenation is identified by the comma in APL and COBOL, a space in SNOBOL, // in PL/I and & in ADA. If the language insists that the length of the referenced object must be specified in the name declaration, then the programmer must see that the sum of both operand lengths matches the length of the result. There is greater flexibility if the length does not have to be declared (SNOBOL). As the length cannot then be determined until run time, due to the unknown length of the actual operand at translation time, these languages require a dynamic storage administration.

Apart from the possibility of access to a complete character string, some programming languages also provide access to parts of the string. These generally take the form of a function reference (PL/I, BASIC). PL/I is taken as an example:

SUBSTR(character__string, index, length)

INDEX(character__string, pattern)

In *SUBSTR* the substring is identified by its start position ('index' characters from the beginning of the string). Conversely, the substring is given as a pattern and *INDEX* reports back the position in which it first appeared. *SUBSTR* can be used at various reference levels: it may also be on the left side of a value assignment if the first parameter is the name of a variable.

SNOBOL permits patterns which are made up from not just one but a set of character strings, and the most important aspect is the facility that the located substring may be replaced:

character__string pattern = substitute__string

It is important to know which string, out of a pattern which contains many, meets with success:

character__string pattern . success__string ...

When one of the character strings of a pattern does meet with success, it is assigned to the name 'success__string'.†

---

† Blatt (1980) has provided an extension of this concept.

7

Compound objects

Compound objects are formed from a suitable combination of given objects which may be either elementary in the context of the programming language under consideration, or already in compound form. To operate with the objects, a description containing the following information must be given, either for each individual object or for each class of objects, all the members of which have an identical structure (compound mode): (1) the composition rules indicating the form of access to the individual components, (2) the mode and number of components which determine the size (storage requirements) of the object, and provide for a check on whether the components are being correctly used from a syntactic point of view, and (3) the identification of selectors which allows components to be addressed individually.

Design specifications offer three alternatives which can lead to different types of access. (1) The most common is the regular structure with random access (arrays, records). (2) LISP is the only language which incorporates, as standard, tree structures with access along the branches; it is the only method of composition in this language. (c) Structures in which access is only possible at 'actual' points (stack, queue, etc) play a part in many applications in computer science. Such structures are not provided as standard in many programming languages but, in the more recent languages which incorporate mode declarations, the programmer can enter them himself. Sequential files, which will be discussed later on, also belong to this latter group.

In the case of random access, each component of a compound object can be addressed directly. One condition required in this case is that selectors, which together with object identifiers form the component identification, are assigned uniquely to the components. Many programming languages have two mechanisms for this: (1) the selector set is an interval of the integers (subscripts), and (2) the selectors are identifiers chosen arbitrarily.

If subscripts are used to select the components, then the objects are referred to as arrays. They are often used in conjunction with loop statements where the same rule for computing a value is applied to the various array elements: in this case, the loop variable runs through the selector set. The specification that all components of an array must be of the same type (homogeneous compound objects) fits in with this use. As the subscript sequence is the only significant aspect in many applications, it is not absolutely essential that integers are used.† It is sufficient to have an arbitrary ordered object set (enumerated mode). This facility, which is offered by PASCAL and some of its successors, enables a problem oriented formulation of loop statements as opposed to the method of coding by integers: *FOR day := monday TO friday ...*

Access via identifiers is most common with heterogeneous compound objects. In general these identifiers are usually specified in the object or mode declarations. The tables in SNOBOL and the sets in SETL‡, where the selectors are not determined until run time, i.e. when the components are entered in the object, form an exception. Some programming language books refer to such objects as structures, others as records. The well-known *COMMON* blocks in FORTRAN can also be seen as records but do in fact have another function.

7.1 Arrays

If elementary objects form the components of an array, this is a one-dimensional array (vector). Multi-dimensional arrays result when the vector components are themselves arrays. In order to address a component of a multi-dimensional array, each dimension requires a subscript. Therefore, the number of subscripts must match the number of dimensions.§

In the more recent programming languages, the number of dimensions is unrestricted. However, the restrictions imposed by some very widely-used languages seldom hinder the programmer: FORTRAN allows three-dimensional arrays at the most; BASIC incorporates one- and two-dimensional arrays with numeric components and one-dimensional ones with alphabetic characters; COBOL allows three-dimensional arrays, the components of which may be both elementary objects (numeric, characters, strings) and also structures.

Array components are normally stored in successive storage cells. Multi-dimensional arrays, for example,

$$array_{11} \quad array_{12} \quad array_{13} \quad array_{14} \quad array_{15}$$
$$array_{21} \quad array_{22} \quad array_{23} \quad array_{24} \quad array_{25}$$
$$array_{31} \quad array_{32} \quad array_{33} \quad array_{34} \quad array_{35}$$

can be stored in rows or columns. Row storage means that, in the above example, the component $array_{21}$ is stored after $array_{15}$ etc., whereas in column storage, the sequence would be $array_{21}$ after $array_{11}$, $array_{12}$ after $array_{31}$, etc.

---

† Obviously it is different if the subscripts are used to carry out more complicated arithmetic operations than transferring to successive elements.
‡ See section 7.7.
§ PL/I is an exception, but allowing one-dimensional access to two-dimensional arrays can cause programming errors.

The sequence chosen is only of importance to the programmer if the programming language offers the possibility of addressing an area of storage in various ways: APL, COBOL and PL/I offer row storage, i.e. the final subscript runs its range of values completely before the last but one is raised by 1; FORTRAN has column storage, i.e. the initial subscript runs its range of values before the second subscript is raised again. The programmer using BLISS can determine the sequence himself.

A storage mapping function is required to provide access to a specific component. For the sake of simplicity, this can be illustrated for the two-dimensional row-storage case:

$$address\,(array_{ij}) = address\,(array_{u1,u2}) + l\cdot\{(i-u_1)\cdot(o_2-u_2+1) + (j-u_2)\}$$

In this case u_k is the lower and o_k the upper limit for the k th subscript and l is the amount of storage required for each individual component. In general l is equal to at least 1. Several components may be stored together, but only when array components require less space than the size of one storage cell. The programmer can explicitly prescribe this in PASCAL or COBOL, for example, but he does not normally need to become involved with the storage mapping function as the compiler usually applies it in the required places.

ALGOL 60	*simpletype ARRAY array [1:3, 1:5];*
FORTRAN 77	a) *simpletype array (1:3, 1:5)*
	b) *DIMENSION array (1:3, 1:5)*
	simpletype array
PL/1	*DECLARE array (1:3, 1:5) type*
ALGOL 68	*[1:3, 1:5] type array*
PASCAL	*array: ARRAY [1:3, 1:5] OF type*
COBOL	*01 array*
	02 line OCCURS 3 TIMES
	03 column OCCURS 5 TIMES type
BASIC	*DIM a(3,5)*
APL	*array← 3 5 ρ initialization*
SNOBOL	*array = ARRAY ('3, 5', initialization)*

Fig. 7.1 Declaration or generation of an example array in various languages. (The BASIC example is based on numeric components.)

The declaration of an array must contain the information needed to establish an object description. Fig. 7.1 shows the declaration of our example array in the various programming languages. *Type* or *simpletype* refers to the component mode. If the lower limit has been specified, the language will permit values other than 1. BASIC normally begins with 0 which can be changed to a lower limit of 1 by *OPTION BASE 1*. APL and SNOBOL do not have declarations; arrays are created by generation operations carried out at run time when the components are at the same time initialized. This is done in SNOBOL using a unique value and arbitrarily in APL.

The systems implementation language BLISS gives the programmer the opportunity to be responsible for the storage mapping function:

STRUCTURE array5[i,j] = (.array5 +(.i − 1)* 5 + (.j − 1));
LOCAL field[20];
MAP array5 field;

The STRUCTURE declaration fixes the storage mapping function, which is then linked to a storage range by MAP. Only its size is indicated in the actual array declaration. In this way, structures other than rectangular ones can be declared, e.g. triangular matrices (Wulf *et al.* 1971).

7.2 Array operations

A distinction must be made between operations on components, the selection of components or component groups, the formation of new arrays and requests for array properties.

Very few programming languages incorporate operations to process all array components without the programmer having to program a loop. In PL/I, all operations defined for scalar operands are also possible for arrays, in which case they are carried out component by component and in the sequence given by row storage.† Arrays may be combined with arrays or with scalar quantities; in the second instance, each array element is combined individually with the scalar quantity. As all operations are carried out component by component, multiplication of two matrices does not correspond to mathematically-based matrix multiplication. (As in PL/I, all operations in APL are extended component by component.)

In comparison, BASIC still uses the matrix operations used in mathematics. The sum, product and difference of matrices and the multiplication of matrices by scalars all have the usual meaning. One-dimensional arrays are always given as column vectors, so that multiplication can be performed with a matrix on the right but the scalar product of two vectors is not possible; the standard function DOT is used for this purpose. Other standard functions are TRN and INV for determining the transposed and inverse matrices respectively, DET for calculating the determinant, and ZER(N,M), CON(N,M), and IDN(N,N) to produce a null matrix, a matrix in which all components are 1, and a unit matrix respectively. The notation for statements containing matrix operations corresponds to that for scalar quantities but the LET is replaced by the MAT symbol.

The selection of subarrays is an important aspect for many applications involving multi-dimensional arrays. In PL/I and APL, only whole rows or columns (e.g. higher dimension subarrays) can be selected. In PL/I, the subscript, which must be varied to select the subarray components, is characterized by an asterisk: array (2, *), in APL it is omitted: array[2;]. In both cases, the second row of the array is selected. ALGOL 68 also leaves out the corresponding subscript: array[2,]. Over and above this, part rows and/or part columns may also be selected: array [3:5, 2:7] selects from a larger array the part where the row subscript moves between 3 and 5 and the column subscript between 2 and 7. ALGOL 68 also introduced the facility for giving

---

† When combining an array with one of its actual components, this sequence is important.

these subarrays new lower limits: *array* [*3:5 AT 1, 2:7 AT 0*] means that the subscript counting in the selected subarray begins with 0 and 1 respectively.

In all programming languages, the components of an array can be combined by means of a loop. If the programming language offers special operators for this purpose, these can often be more effectively implemented. PL/I incorporates as standard functions *PROD(array)* and *SUM(array)* which form the product or sum of all array components respectively.

In order to combine array elements by arbitrary operations, APL uses three mechanisms which are independent of the operations used: reduction, internal product, and external product.† Reduction *q/array* combines all array elements with each other via operator *q*. For example, + */array* forms the sum of all elements. Care should be taken with the non-associative operations: for example, − */1 2 3 4*; as APL evaluates expressions from right to left, this corresponds to *1 − (2 − (3 − 4))*. In the case of multi-dimensional arrays, reduction in respect of an arbitrary dimension can take place: *q/[k]array*. The dimension of the result is 1 below that of the given array.

The internal product *f1 p.q f2* is defined such that the operation *q* is carried out component by component with arrays *f1* and *f2* and then reduced by operation *p*. $a + . \times b$ is thus the scalar product of two vectors *a* and *b*: $a_1 b_1 + a_2 b_2 + \ldots + a_n b_n$. The external product corresponds to the cartesian product: *f1 ∘.q f2*. In this case, all elements of *f1* are combined with elements of *f2* via operation *q*, thus forming a higher dimension array. For example, if *a* is a vector with numbers 1 to 10 as components, then *a∘.× a* yields a multiplication table.

Value assignment to arrays can obviously be carried out component by component, but can also be done, in many languages, for the whole array by means of initialization and input statements. Constant array identifications, as required for other value assignments, are seldom found, especially in the most widely used languages. For example, ALGOL 68 and ADA have aggregates for this purpose, that is a bracketed list of constants, e.g. *((1,2,3), (4,5,6))* for a 2 × 3 matrix. ADA has an extended notation with subscript or subscript range information: *(1..n => (1 => 1.0, 2..n => 0.0))* describes an *n* × *n* matrix with a first column containing 1.0 and the other columns 0.0. In APL, the binary operator *ρ* produces arrays, *b ρ a* means that an array is formed from the elements of *a* with a dimension vector *b*:

2 3 ρ 1 2 3 4 5 6   produces a 2 × 3 matrix,
4 4 ρ 1 0 0 0 0   produces a 4 × 4 unit matrix†

Conversely, the unary operator *ρ* gives a dimension vector, i.e. the upper limit for any subscript position. (Two-fold application *ρρ array* gives the number of elements in the dimension vector and hence the dimension.)

7.3 Records

Objects with components of different modes are involved in many applications; personnel data could be taken as an example. Only the older programming

---

† Iverson (1979) has outlined further mechanisms more recently.
† If the elements of the right operand are not enough they are cyclically repeated.

languages and those oriented towards other fields of application do not involve records (ALGOL 60, FORTRAN, APL, LISP, BASIC). In records, selectors are a sequence of identifiers which can be chosen arbitrarily but are fixed at translation time. Like the subscripts of arrays, selectors can be used in any sequence in processing statements; thus access to the components remains arbitrary. As the declaration of a compound object assigns the mode of the selected component to each selector at translation time, the statements in which components occur can also be checked for syntactic correctness.

Programming languages offer two notation alternatives for the declaration of record modes and record objects: bracket notation or level notation. The example in Fig. 7.2 declares an object with the identification *wageslip*, the components of which are also record objects. *Name, time* and *wage* are used as selectors. PL/I and COBOL, which do not allow mode declarations, use level notation in which the structuring of an object is clarified by the level number: all components of an object or of a subobject have the same level number and

(a) Example of a record object:

Wageslip					
name		*time*		*wage*	
surname	*forename*	*normal*	*overtime*	*normal*	*overtime*

(b) Declaration in PL/1 (object declaration):

```
DECLARE 1 wageslip,
        2 name,
          3 surname CHARACTER (15),
          3 forename CHARACTER (10),
        2 time,
          3 normal DECIMAL FIXED (4,1),
          3 overtime DECIMAL FIXED (4,1),
        2 wage,
          3 normal DECIMAL FIXED (6,2),
          3 overtime DECIMAL FIXED (6,2),
```

(c) Declaration in PASCAL (mode declaration):
```
TYPE modewageslip =
  RECORD
    name: RECORD
          surname: PACKED ARRAY [1..15] OF CHAR;
          forename: PACKED ARRAY [1..10] OF CHAR
          END;
    time: RECORD
          normal: REAL;
          overtime: REAL
          END;
    wage: RECORD
          normal: REAL;
          overtime: REAL
          END
  END;
```

Fig. 7.2 Record objects.

this must be greater than that of the subobject itself. Whereas the level numbers in PL/I can be chosen arbitrarily, COBOL fixes them to lie between 01 and 49. In the bracket notation, the components of a sub-object are enclosed by bracketing symbols, for example *RECORD* and *END* in PASCAL.

The selectors for the components of an object or of a sub-object must obviously be different, but the same selectors can be used again in different objects or subobjects. In general, any mode allowed in the language considered can be used as a component mode; this also applies for record and array modes. If the language allows mode declarations, the programmer has the choice between a detailed description of component modes and the use of self-defined mode indications. In PL/I, which does not allow mode declarations, the *LIKE* construction provides an abbreviated form: *DECLARE newwageslip LIKE wageslip.*

If record objects or parts of them are used in statements, then not only the objects but the required components too must be specified. In COBOL and ALGOL 68, one must proceed level by level from selected components to the total object: *normal OF time OF wageslip,* whereas the other languages begin with the total object: *wageslip.time.normal.* The ALGOL family require all necessary levels to be entered† whereas COBOL and PL/I leave out the higher levels when the next selector is unique. (This may have disastrous consequences in later program modifications, as is the case with all such arrangements allowed for the convenience of the programmer).

7.4 Record mode matching

In value assignments, all the languages mentioned can process individual components, substructures and whole objects. Obviously, the name of a variable must be on the left side, and the reference to the mode on the right. This involves the problem of deciding when the modes of two records are equal. Whereas ALGOL 68 and PL/I give a very broad definition of equality, most other languages (e.g. PASCAL and ADA) work within more confined specifications. Ichbiah *et al.* (1979) have provided details of the various alternatives:

(1) Each new record mode declaration introduces a new mode which is different from those already defined. ADA prefers this narrow solution. It facilitates both language implementation and program legibility.

(2) Two record modes are regarded as equal if selector identification and component modes are in agreement. The only difference between this definition and the first one is that the same record mode can be entered in the program several times.‡ This is of interest if the record mode is not explicitly declared but entered as part of object declarations. The same mode is intuitively awarded to the objects

---

† PASCAL permits a shortened form of statements related to certain records, with the construction *WITH recordlist DO BEGIN ...END.*
‡ The definition may also be written in full the first time and abbreviated the next (e.g. *a,b: real*).

```
object1: RECORD            object: RECORD
       a: real;                  a: real;
       b: real;                  b: real;
    END                       END;
```

but according to the strict first definition, they are not equal.

(3) Selector identifications do not have to agree, but component modes do. This definition corresponds to the mathematical concept of record objects as elements of a cartesian product. The same definition also regards an

   object3: RECORD x,y: real; END

as having the same mode as the above declared objects.

(4) Selectors and component modes must agree but the sequence does not have to. This corresponds to the mathematical concept of record objects as trees with labelled edges. The COBOL statement

   MOVE CORRESPONDING object1 TO object2

and the PL/I statement

   object2 = object1, BY NAME†

are based on this concept which is, however, not used consistently in these languages.

So far, no definition of equality of component modes has been given. It may be narrowly defined, in which case identification has to agree, or it may be defined in a much wider sense by using the same definition again; the definition is then recursive. ALGOL 68 chooses this latter alternative.

If arrays and records occur in nested form then the equality definition can be carried so far that an array of records and a 'similarly' constructed record of arrays are regarded as having the same mode (PL/I):

```
DECLARE 1a(6),    or    DECLARE 1a,
       2 b,                   2 b(6),
       2 c                    2 c(6).
```

(From a mathematical point of view, in this case even non-isomorphic trees are lumped together.)

7.5 Aggregates and record modes with variants

If a newly composed constant is to be assigned to a record variable rather than the actual referenced object of another variable, then suitable notation must be available to cover this. These constants are known as aggregates.‡

ADA has a very flexible method of dealing with this and hence will be used here as a basis for discussion. In general, an aggregate consists of a bracketed list of constants in which pre-evaluated variables and expressions are permitted:

   schedule: CONSTANT week

      := (true, true, true, true, true, false, false)

Assignment of the components of the object *schedule* is then carried out in the

---

† In this case, the same component of *object1* is assigned to each one of *object2* having the same selector.

‡ For example, in ALGOL 68, *structure display*.

prescribed sequence (positional notation). Alternatively, assignment can take place by explicit selection and in this case the sequence is arbitrary:

schedule: CONSTANT week
:= (mo .. fr = > true, OTHERS = > false)

or   schedule: CONSTANT week
:= (sa | so = > false, OTHERS = > true)

As COBOL record objects are not only used as working data but also as input/output data, special components are required for the format. Fig. 7.3 shows an output object: the components which are irrelevant for the algorithm are labelled with the special selector *FILLER*. A (constant) value is specified in the declaration for these components. (There is no specification in the input data; any characters in the corresponding positions on the input medium are ignored.)

```
01   wageslipcopy.
     02   name.
          03 surname     PICTURE IS X(15).
          03 FILLER      PICTURE IS X(3) VALUE IS SPACES.
          03 forename    PICTURE IS X(10).

     02   time.
          03 FILLER      PICTURE IS X(8) VALUE IS '⎵⎵time:⎵'.
          03 normal      PICTURE IS ZZ9.9.
          03 FILLER      PICTURE IS X(5) VALUE IS '⎵ and ⎵'.
          03 overtime    PICTURE IS ZZ9.9.
          03 FILLER      PICTURE IS X(11) VALUE IS '⎵overtime ⎵⎵'.

     02   wage.
          03 FILLER      PICTURE IS X VALUE IS '£   '.
          03 normal      PICTURE IS ZZZ9.99.
          03 FILLER      PICTURE IS X(4) VALUE IS '⎵ + ⎵ £   '.
          03 overtime    PICTURE IS ZZZ9.99.
```

Fig. 7.3   Record object with constant components in COBOL.

A number of compound objects, in which individual components are recorded with different meanings in order to save storage space, are often involved: for instance, a company's personnel data may have a Boolean component which means *pregnant* in the case of women and *conscripted* for men. In this example, a sufficiently complicated selector (e.g. *pregnant_ or_conscripted*) is chosen but structural differences are no longer clear.

In FORTRAN, *EQUIVALENCE* can be used to assist provided that the modes of both alternatives are compatible (see chapter 8); COBOL allows various record structures to be assigned to the same input/output object and the structure of working objects to be defined many times using *REDEFINES*. The problem with these solutions is that different access paths are defined independently of each referenced object. Hence access may be via the wrong path, without necessarily involving an error message. (For example, the selector *pregnant* can be used even though the referenced object concerns a man's data.) A systematic solution must regard the relevant record structure as an inherent property of the referenced object, and this would mean that access could be checked for acceptability at run time at least. PASCAL and its successors opt for the record mode with structure variants: a separate structure is defined in the mode declaration for each subset of objects by a case discrimination clause and this means that both different selectors and different substructures can occur (Fig. 7.4). Notation for the ADA concept (Ichbiah *et al.*, 1979) makes implementation especially clear: a labelled component (discriminant) contains a constant value for the object in question, which controls interpretation of the variable part. This component is part of the common section:

sex : CONSTANT (male, female)

(a) PASCAL:
TYPE sex = (male, female);
TYPE person = RECORD common__part;
    CASE sex OF
        male: (special__part__1);
        female: (special__part__2)
END;

(b) ADA:
TYPE sex__type IS (male, female);
TYPE person (sex: sex__type) IS
    RECORD common__part;
        CASE sex OF
            WHEN male => special__part__1;
            WHEN female =>special__part__2;
        END CASE
    END RECORD;

(c) ALGOL 68:
MODE maleperson = STRUCTURE (common__part,
                    special__part__1);
MODE femaleperson = STRUCTURE (common__part,
                    special__part__2);
MODE person = UNION (maleperson, femaleperson);

Fig. 7.4   Record modes with variants.

The mathematical background is more obvious in ALGOL 68 and SIMULA 67:† with such record mode declarations, it is basically a question of the union of many different record modes which are brought together to form a union mode.

In addition to case discrimination, iteration is a basic concept of information processing. In the case of record modes with structure variants, this leads to a component-controlled repetition of another component. So far, this concept does not seem to have found favour in programming languages. ALGOL 68 recognizes arrays with flexible limits as record components, but the limits are not themselves components (although they can be checked). In ADA the discriminant may be used as the array limit of a component, but it must be

---

† Transfer from class to superior class.

68

specified not only in the constant declaration but also in the declaration of the variable name.†

7.6 Recursive record modes

Most programming languages do not allow the newly defined record mode to occur again as component mode in its own definition. Of the languages with independent mode declarations, only ADA accepts this possibility, whilst the others allow only pointers to objects of the same mode as components. However, the recursive record mode is already quite an old concept: apart from the elementary objects (atoms), LISP allows as record objects only lists which can be understood to be a recursive record mode: each object consists of two components with the selectors *CAR* and *CDR*. The first component is again an atom or a list, the second is a list. Fig. 7.5 shows such an object and the PASCAL transcription of a record mode declaration for LISP objects.

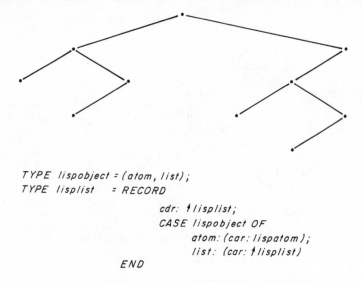

```
TYPE lispobject = (atom, list);
TYPE lisplist   = RECORD

                  cdr: ↑lisplist;
                  CASE lispobject OF
                       atom: (car: lispatom);
                       list: (car: ↑lisplist)
           END
```

Fig. 7.5 Example of a LISP object (branches with empty lists are omitted) and PASCAL record mode declaration for LISP objects.

As the objects are potentially infinite in size, assignment of a defined reference object is only possible if an undefined object, which ends recursion on individual branches, exists explicitly, for example:

subobject.car := atom1; subobject.cdr := NIL; ...
subobject.cdr.car := atom2; subobject.cdr.cdr := NIL

The storage requirements of an object depend on the number of levels at which value assignments have been carried out, and is therefore not constant. When a variable is generated, future storage needed for the reference object cannot be predicted. The PASCAL transcription shows how these objects can be

---

† Different sizes of referenced objects are possible if an *access type* is used.

implemented: if objects of the same mode are required to be components, a pointer is used instead of the objects themselves.

The binary trees in LISP are just one variant of the linked lists which are involved in various fields of computer science, and can be implemented with recursive record modes. Other examples are stacks and queues where changes take place only at the ends of the list. General lists, where insertions and deletions are possible at all points may be linked in one way or both directions (forward and backward) play an important part in sorting problems. Denert and Franck (1977) describe a number of algorithms suitable for this purpose which make use of recursive record types.

7.7 Special cases

SNOBOL patterns are compound objects which allow deviation from the tree structure. They are formed from character strings and previously constructed patterns by concatenation and other alternatives: Fig. 7.6 shows a pattern describing a character string of the form

jan, 01   jan, 02   aug, 01

amongst others.†

Patterns can be used to test whether a substring, which matches one of the pattern alternatives, occurs in a character string:

characterstring pattern

and also to replace the newly discovered substring by another, and even an empty one if necessary:

characterstring pattern = newsubstring

It is possibly important to the program continuation to know which alternative

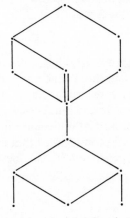

```
month = 'jan' / 'jun' / 'jul' / 'aug'
day   = '01' / '02' / '12' / '13'
date  = 'month', 'day'
```

Fig. 7.6   SNOBOL pattern and graphic interpretation.

---

† The pattern can also be represented as a tree, by replacing the junction with suitably frequent repetition of the substructure.

was successful during the search for a matched substring, especially when the pattern consists of various alternatives. To this end, the programmer can attach a variable to whole patterns or pattern components to which the successfully located alternative is assigned as reference object:

date = month . discoveredmonth ',' day

Note that the value assignment itself does not come from the pattern definition but from the search operation (as an implicit value assignment). If discovered components are to be indicated even if the whole search operation has met with no success, the dollar sign should be used instead of the full stop.

The *TABLE* construction in SNOBOL can be considered as a one-dimensional array with arbitrary selectors which need not be specified until run time.† Using *t = TABLE(n,m)* an array of initial size *n* can be generated which can subsequently be lengthened by *m* elements if the space is too small. The individual elements are picked up by *t<selector>*. If there is still no component for that selector, then it is generated and initialized by the empty character string. The *TABLE* construction can also be regarded as a set, the elements of which are pairs. However, the fact that no set-theoretical operations exist, and the function of both components is different, contradicts this view. SETL incorporates the set as a compound object (Schwartz, 1975). In this language, *n*-tuples $(x_1, x_2 ..., x_n)$ can be formed from arbitrary components; all set-theoretical operations such as union, intersection, and tests for subsets or element membership relation exist.

PASCAL and some languages derived from it incorporate the possibility of a restricted set concept: subsets can be formed from the elements of a fixed finite set which may be given as a set of elements from an enumerated mode, or as an interval of integers:

TYPE basiccolour = (red, yellow, blue);
TYPE colour = SET OF basiccolour;
VAR c: colour;
c: = [yellow, red]

The objects of such a mode are clearly characterized by those elements from the base set which belong to it and those which do not. From this, a very efficient implementation emerges as a record object with Boolean components, the number of which correspond to the number of elements in the base set. The disadvantage of this concept is that the elements in the base set must be fixed at translation time. Hence, it is recommended that a combination of the flexible SETL concept with the efficient PASCAL one should be used (Schneider, 1980).

---

† The mode conversion *CONVERT*, in which the selectors become the first column of an array is a reason for the array interpretation.

8

Data control

Five operations are explicitly or implicitly available to the programmer for dealing with programming language objects.

(1) In general, assignment of an identifier to an object occurs explicitly by a declaration at the beginning of the range of the object. Even the identification in the implicit declarations of FORTRAN, which appears part way through the range, must not obscure the true validity range.

(2) The assignment may be relinquished implicitly by leaving a range of validity, or by assigning another object to the same identification. This relinquishing process need not be final, i.e. the programming language can allow that the previous assignment may be reproduced at a later stage.

(3) The creation of the programming language object need not coincide with the assignment of an identifier. The point in time at which the object is created is much more dependent on the storage administration that is used, but it may be left explicitly to the programmer, too.

(4) The same applies for deletion of a programming language object.

(5) A programming language object can only be used between creation and deletion points, but does not necessarily depend on assignment of an identification to it. Access may also be via a pointer. This fact shows clearly that a difference must be made between the validity range of an identification, the existence range of an object, and the access range.

8.1 Validity, existence and access range

Validity range is related to the identification of programming language objects: it is limited by the assignment of an identifier to an object on the one hand, and the relinquishing of this assignment on the other. As the assignment is usually established by a declaration, it may also be known as the declaration range.

If the use of identifiers is to be translated completely during syntax analysis, the validity range of each identifier must be specified at translation time (static validity range). In this case, each identifier does not need its own validity range, but a common one can be given to groups of identifiers. This means that the ranges are limited either by specially determined language constructs (e.g. ALGOL 60: *BEGIN, END*) or are linked with other language constructs which are basically used for another purpose and define the validity range as a secondary effect (e.g. FORTRAN: *SUBROUTINE, END*; ALGOL 68: all control statements). With the more recent language developments, the trend is towards declaration of each identifier at the beginning of its range and for no identifier to appear repeatedly within a validity range.†

In dynamic validity ranges, each application of an identifier relates to the last assignment made to an object in the program run. Hence, whether the identifier picks up an array, a procedure, or a simple variable is not known at translation time; processing can only be done by interpretation. LISP belongs in this category as do APL and SNOBOL, with certain limitations.

The existence range relates to the internal object: it is limited on one side by the creation of a programming language object and on the other by its deletion. Hence this concept is important at program run time. Existence ranges and their mutual position allowed in a programming language are largely responsible for determining the expenditure which must be made on storage administration. The existence range of an object and the validity range of its identifier must not coincide as is evident in almost all programming languages. In FORTRAN 77 programs, validity range matches a program unit (main program, subprogram), but using the *SAVE* specification, the existence range matches the total program run time. In ALGOL 60 programs, validity range (block) can be restricted by the block contained in it. This does in fact happen when the same identifier is used for another object; the original object still exists and becomes accessible once again after leaving the internal block. In LISP programs, the existence range begins with object creation (e.g. by *CONS, LIST, SETQ*) and ends at the point where access is no longer possible.‡

A distinction is made between static existence ranges (e.g. in FORTRAN, BASIC, COBOL), dynamic existence ranges which are automatically administered (block structure in the ALGOL family and PL/I), and dynamic existence ranges which are explicitly administered. In the latter, the programming language contains instructions for creating objects (PL/I, PASCAL, ALGOL 68, SIMULA, LISP, etc.) and also for deleting them if necessary (PL/I). In general, no explicit identifiers have to be present for the objects being created—pointers are quite sufficient.

The access range is the part of a program in which an object can be used in statements. In the classical languages such as ALGOL 60, FORTRAN, and

---

† Labels which are declared at a later point, and selectors which may be used repeatedly form an exception to this rule.

‡ Fischer (1972) and Simon (1976) have shown that the effectiveness of LISP is not impaired by leaving out *CONS*, but storage administration is simplified as a result.

COBOL, the access range matches the validity range because each object can only be picked up by the identifier assigned to it. If the access range extends beyond the validity range of the object declaration, then higher reference level names must exist to allow the object to be picked up without using its identifier. This pointer technique is absolutely necessary if the application requires a previously unknown number of objects (list processing).

However, the fact that this division between access range on the one hand and existence and validity range on the other leads to problems should not be overlooked:

(1) If the referenced object is subject to automatic storage administration, or the programming language provides explicit instructions for deleting the object (ALGOL 68, PL/I), then the validity range of the pointer declaration can extend further than the existence of the object. A so-called dangling reference is formed.

(2) If the existence range of the referenced object is neither terminated automatically nor explicitly, then the memory becomes filled with an increasing number of objects to which access becomes impossible (*heap* in ALGOL 68, LISP, SIMULA, SNOBOL). A costly garbage collection is then required, during the course of which all possible access paths are investigated.

To overcome the first problem, PASCAL and its successors permit pointers only to objects which have no explicit identifier and hence cannot be explicitly deleted. This also ensures that the existence range of the referenced object terminates not later than that of the pointer. If an upper limit for the required storage area is given in the pointer mode declaration, this area can be relinquished totally on leaving the existence range of the pointer.†

8.2 Block structure

In the ALGOL family of languages, the blocks control both the valid range of identifiers and the object existence range. Blocks may follow in sequence or be nested (see Fig. 8.1).

There is no upper limit set on the depth of nesting. Basically, each identifier is valid only within the block in which it is declared.

As the same identifier can be used in various blocks for different objects, a more precise rule is necessary: (1) If an object is declared in a block,‡ then it does not exist outside this block, and the reference to the identifier is invalid. (2) If an object is declared in a block and a block contained within it (internal block) has no object declaration with the same identifier, then the internal block 'inherits' the declaration; the identifier is valid and identifies the same object as in the external block. (3) If an object is declared in a block and an inner block contains a new object declaration with the same identifier, the object in the internal block is regarded as a different one: the object declared in the

---

† This quantity option is preferred by ADA as a result of possible applications in which time plays a critical part.

‡ Procedures are also regarded as blocks.

```
 0    BEGIN  INTEGER i;
 1        PROCEDURE a...
 2        BEGIN INTEGER m; INTEGER n;
 3            PROCEDURE b...
 4            BEGIN REAL n;...
 5        c:      BEGIN INTEGER n;
 6                    ... i := i + 1 ...
 7                END;
 8                ... d; ...
 9            END;
10            PROCEDURE d;
11            BEGIN REAL m; REAL ARRAY f[...];...
12            END;
13            INTEGER i;
14            ... e; ...
15        END;
16        PROCEDURE e...
17        BEGIN INTEGER n; REAL i;
18        f:      BEGIN...
19            g:      BEGIN REAL ARRAY f[...];...
20                    END;
21                END;
22        END;
23    END;
```

Fig. 8.1   Block structure in the ALGOL family. The dots indicate statements.

outer block cannot be reached in the internal block although it does still exist.‡
Fig. 8.2 shows the block labels in which each declaration from Fig. 8.1 is valid.
The block structure has the advantage that statement sequences can be entered
or modified without the locally declared objects and operations carried out on
them having any effect outside the block.

The example of Fig. 8.1 shows a special feature resulting from the fact that
the declarations in a block can occur in arbitrary sequence in most programming languages: the identifiers i (line 6), d (line 8), and e (line 14) are used even
before their declaration. This not only impairs the legibility of the program, but
also prevents it being translated in one pass. In most cases, a suitable reordering
can be effected, but there are two language structures which do not allow this:
(1) In indirect recursive procedures, one procedure calls a second which recalls
the first one again. There are useful applications for this type of case, e.g. in

---

‡ Obviously the object can still be reached using a pointer declared in the outer block.

| Declaration | | Validity range | | | | | | | |
line	symbol	global	a	b	c	d	e	f	g
0	i	*							
1	a	*	*	*	*	*	*	*	*
2	m		*	*	*				
2	n		*			*			
3	b		*	*	*	*			
4	n		*						
5	c		*	*					
5	n		*						
10	d		*	*	*	*			
11	m					*			
11	f					*			
13	i		*	*	*	*			
16	e	*	*	*	*	*	*	*	*
17	n						*	*	*
17	i						*	*	*
18	f						*	*	
19	g							*	*
19	f								*

Fig. 8.2   Validity ranges for Fig. 8.1.†

compiler construction. (2) In the context of forward jumps, the GO TO statement in which the label is used occurs before the label is reached. From the point of view of structured programming, there is no real objection to this type of jump. PASCAL and some of the languages influenced by it (EUCLID, ADA) demand that the identifiers of procedures be declared before their use and in this case the procedure body may still be missing; PASCAL requires the same of all labels.

If implicit declarations coincide with block structure (PL/I), then the question arises as to which block the declaration is valid in. PL/I chooses the outermost procedure in which the corresponding statement is contained; as long as labels are involved, the innermost block is its validity range.

8.3 Deviations from block structure

The simplest specification for the extent of a validity range for identifiers consists of identifying the validity range of all identifiers as the whole program. This regulation is found in COBOL, SNOBOL and the versions of BASIC which do not allow compile-time procedures.

Division of all identifiers into local and global ones is also easy: as a result of one declaration (explicit or implicit), globally valid identifiers can be used in the whole program, whereas the validity range of local identifiers is restricted to specific language structure areas. FORTRAN, APL and BASIC‡ are examples

---

† In ALGOL 60 f is not a block, but a compound statement which defines no special validity range.
‡ Most assembler languages fall into this category, too.

of this. In these languages, procedure identifiers are universally valid as are the identifiers of *COMMON* blocks in FORTRAN (this does not include identifiers for objects contained in them). On the other hand identifiers of all other declared objects are only locally valid in the procedure in which they are included. It is typical of this ruling that all non-local identifiers are global, and hence there is no possibility of giving a validity range to identifiers which cover several procedures but which are not global. BLISS mixes both principles—*LOCAL* declarations are subject to block structure and *GLOBAL* declarations are also possible.

Although PL/I assumes the block concept basically, it does have the facility of importing declarations from any other blocks. Declaration then takes place in all validity ranges and is supplied with the option *EXTERNAL*. For example, in Fig. 8.1, the declaration of f in lines 11 and 19 could have this attribute. The reason for this construction is the declaration of files via which program parts can communicate with each other.

Block structure offers protection against undesired use of identifiers in one direction only: identifiers declared internally cannot be used externally. Further demands were made with the development of modular programming: (1) Automatic transmission of declarations to an internal block must be suppressable. (2) Identifiers must be able to be imported into a validity range, from a parallel one if necessary. (3) It must be possible to specify restriction or import limits both at the point where the objects are declared and in the place where they are or are not needed. These demands have been met to a different extent by all programming languages that allow module structure.

EUCLID distinguishes between open and closed validity ranges. In contrast to the blocks, which are open validity ranges, the closed validity ranges (modules and procedure bodies) do not automatically inherit the declarations of the surrounding validity range. However (1) declarations can be made to be automatically inherited by using the option *PERVASIVE*, and (2) identifiers can be imported by an *IMPORTS* clause as long as they have been released by the exporting module with an *EXPORTS* clause. In comparison, MODULA recognizes only the export/import mechanism (Geissmann, 1979). In this case, each procedure defines the existence range of objects which are local and hence declared in the declaration part. The declaration part can also contain module declarations. The module has a structure similar to procedures (declarations to which procedures and modules can belong, and statements), but a different interpretation: it defines no new existence range; the objects declared in the module exist in the surrounding procedure. However, the module certainly defines its own validity range, so that the objects declared in it are not apparent outside as long as they are not explicitly exported.

8.4 Storage management

Storage management is decisively influenced by the existence range of objects created in the program. In addition to this, however, the program and other data also require storage space: (1) In the case of very extensive programs, program parts required later can take over the storage space of program parts which are no longer needed (overlay). It would be useful if future programming languages could formulate these properties in a way that would not be dependent on the operating system used. (2) Intermediate results occur both during expression evaluation and during parameter passing. The number of these results cannot always be determined at translation time—recursive procedures are a case in point. (3) Administration information must be preserved. Return addresses of subroutines, re-entry points of coroutines, control information of tasks, and storage mapping functions all belong in this category.

If the above-mentioned overlaying of program parts is disregarded for the moment and the existence ranges of objects created in the program is considered, then three cases of storage management can be distinguished: static storage management, dynamic storage management by a stack, and dynamic storage management on a heap.

Static storage administration can be used in both FORTRAN and COBOL: in COBOL because all objects exist during the whole period of the program run, and in FORTRAN because the lack of recursive procedures enables a fixed storage range to be assigned to each procedure. In these cases, the compiler can treat the storage management as a whole and assign a storage place to each object.

Both block structure and the nested call of procedures lead to a stack-based storage management in so far as the existence range of objects are influenced by these structures. If the program run enters a new existence range, then storage space must be made available for the objects created there. As this existence range is abandoned before the surrounding existence ranges (due to nesting), the storage areas which are occupied last are the first to be released. Fig. 8.3 shows this type of storage management: B1 – B11 give a dynamic representation of the block and call structure, i.e. blocks and procedures appear in the sequence in which they are processed. It is certainly possible for B4, B5 and B6 to be a block (or procedure call) in a cyclic program part, and for B2 (with B3) to be a procedure which is recalled as B9 (with B10). As various storage ranges of different sizes can be assigned to a block (or a procedure) as it re-appears, only part of the storage administration can be processed at translation time: as long as objects require fixed storage amounts,† their storage address can be determined relative to the beginning of the respective range.

If statements for the creation and/or deletion of objects are available in the programming language, then the deletion sequence cannot be determined from the sequence in which the objects were created. This applies irrespective of whether the objects are created by independent statements such as *ALLO-CATE* (PL/I), *NEW* (PASCAL), *HEAP* (ALGOL 68), or by the evaluation of expressions (concatenation in SNOBOL, or value assignment in APL). In contrast to stack-based storage administration, the following problems arise: (1) If the objects are recursive records, then the number of objects cannot be determined at translation time. (2) The objects which are accessible, via variables or pointers declared in a block, do not occupy contiguous storage space. Intermediate objects can be created which belong to a surrounding block. Thus

---

† Hence no dynamic arrays.

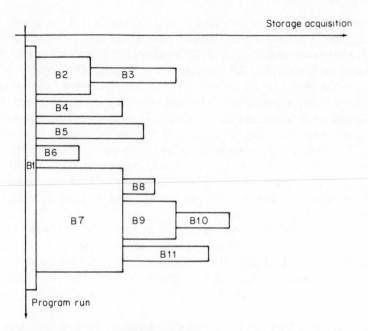

Fig. 8.3   Storage management based on the stack principle.

gaps then occur, between storage parts which are still occupied, when a storage area is abandoned. (3) When leaving the existence range of a pointer, it is not clear whether the referenced object can also be released, or whether another means of access still exists. For these reasons, storage management is not restricted only to the creation and deletion of objects at run time, but also comprises garbage collection from time to time. There are various algorithms for this: Denert and Franck (1977) have provided a good review of the subject.

8.5 Storage allocation statements in FORTRAN

FORTRAN has the capability of two forms of declaration which are relevant to storage management and allow the same storage space to be allocated to various objects. The *EQUIVALENCE* declaration is responsible for the overlay of items within a program unit, and the *COMMON* declaration identifies items in different program units.

The declaration

   COMMON/identifier/variablelist

ensures that the enumerated variables are filed in the identified storage range in the given sequence. If this same identifier is used in a further *COMMON* declaration in the same program unit, then the variables displayed there are attached. This storage space can be picked up by referring to the same identifier in another program unit. The internal objects of a name from each of the first and second program unit are then identical: if a value is assigned to the variable in one program unit, then the corresponding variable in the other program unit has the same value.†

---

† Both variables can be identified differently in both program units.

The size of such a *COMMON* storage area can be calculated as the sum total of the storage space occupied by the individual objects and must be the same in all program units.‡ When objects which differ in size are filed in a *COMMON* range, care must be taken to ensure that the object limits are consistent in the different program units. Thus, FORTRAN 77 does not permit mixing of numeric objects and character strings in the same *COMMON* block.

The argument in favour of the *COMMON* declaration, that the parameter lists in procedures can in this way be kept small, is frequently encountered in FORTRAN literature. However, this only conceals the true interface and does no harm provided that data module simulation, as described by Kimm *et al.* (1979), is involved. In any case, the objects in all program units should be identified in precisely the same manner.

The declaration

EQUIVALENCE (v1, v2, ..., vn)

ensures that the identifiers *v1, v2, ..., vn,* declared in the same program unit, identify the same internal object. In reality, only the name of a single variable, and not of many, is involved (Fig. 8.4). It becomes more complicated when array elements occur in the declaration. This leads to an overlay of all arrays by

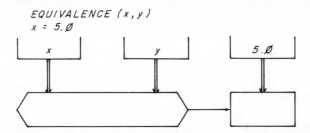

Fig. 8.4 Identification of names from the *EQUIVALENCE* declaration.

identifying not only the internal objects of the specified array elements, but also those of their neighbours. If the involved arrays have different subscript bounds, then the programmer must be fully conversant with storage arrangements because the overlay goes beyond these boundaries. Care must also be taken to ensure that the overlay of arrays is consistent, for example:

EQUIVALENCE (a(1), b(1))
EQUIVALENCE (a(5), c(10))
EQUIVALENCE (c(5), b(10))

is inconsistent because the two last lines mean that *a(1)* is identified with *c(6)* and hence with *b(11)* which is in contradiction to the first line.

It is often said in favour of the *EQUIVALENCE* declaration that 'storage space is saved and the program is nevertheless easy to survey'.† However, *EQUIVALENCE* does have a side effect in value assignments, which certainly does not assist in survey and maintenance. The same effect is achieved much more reliably using the block structure employed by other languages.

‡ This requirement does not apply for *COMMON* blocks with no identification.
† Quotation from a FORTRAN textbook!

9

Elementary flow control

So far, objects, and operations involved with them, have been at the forefront of discussions. The possibilities available to the programmer to influence the operating sequence forms the object of this next section. He can operate at various levels: he can use operator priority for expressions, sequential flow control for statements, and synchronization mechanisms between processes running in parallel for whole programs or program parts.

Programming languages provide a way of combining many operations to form an expression. The sequence in which the individual operations are to be carried out is determined by operator priority and bracket structure.

Within an algorithm described sequentially there are operation sequences which have to be carried out alternately or repeated in cycles. There are also cases in which the elements of an operation sequence can be carried out in arbitrary order (collateral clauses in ALGOL 68, *FOR-ALL* structures for sets); this does not exclude the simultaneous processing of elements on several processors. Procedures and coroutines are also used to formulate sequential algorithms in a clear way.

Coroutines signal the transition of control of processes operating in parallel. In the sequential case, importance is attached to suitable formulation of control structures, but here the main emphasis lies on suitable formulation of communication and synchronization mechanisms.

No other area of programming language has been so hotly disputed as the control of sequential processes. The question as to whether explicit *GO TO* statements are necessary or desirable has been a favourite topic. Arguments for both sides are published in a conference paper by Leavenworth (1972). In the meantime the emphasis has switched from the original argument, as to which control structures are necessary in order to program a specific control flow, towards which ones are suitable for producing a program which is highly legible.†

---

† Compare the cases cited by Knuth (1974) in favour of *GO TO* statements.

The sequential program is characterized by an individual flowline along which one statement can be followed by the next. The classical model of the universal computer (von-Neumann-computer) allows three deviations from this sequence: *GO TO* statement, conditioned branch, and program change (operations with the program as data). The graph theoretical results of Böhm and Jacopini (1966) can be used as theoretical background: they show that each program structure with no cycles involving entry or exit points can be composed from the two-sided alternative, iteration, and concatenation.‡

Clearly structuring can be achieved in hierarchical cooperation by procedures, and in cooperation at the same level by coroutines. Several programming languages also provide structures for formulating non-deterministic branches and for dealing with exceptional cases.

9.1 Operator priority

When many operations are joined together to form an expression, the sequence in which they are to be carried out must be fixed. The same problem has long been apparent to those involved in writing mathematical formulae, so it seems logical that the solution found satisfactory in this latter case should be adopted for the present purposes: a priority level is assigned to each operator; if two operators of different rank coincide, then the higher-ranked one is executed first. Any deviation from the resultant order should be indicated by means of parentheses only. If two operators of the same rank coincide without any parentheses being used, the programming language definition must make clear whether the left or the right operator has priority or whether the decision can be left to the implementor. With a few exceptions, most programming languages opt for left to right ordering but often accept that another sequence may be selected, provided it gives the same result.†

Programming languages do differ in the number of priority levels involved and the ranking of the operators. The range extends from four levels in PASCAL and BASIC up to 12 levels in SNOBOL. LISP, APL and ALGOL 68 are special cases: because of its functional notation, LISP uses no priority rule, APL operates from right to left without any priority, as long as no brackets are used, and ALGOL 68 provides ten levels and the programmer is free to arrange the binary operators in the bottom nine groups as he pleases, whereas the top group is reserved for the unary operator.

With arithmetic operators there are generally three priority levels. Exponentiation is the highest one, followed by the multiplicative operations (multiplication, division, remainder), where once again SNOBOL gives multiplication a higher priority than division. When operations of equal rank coincide, evaluation is from left to right. There are exceptions relating to exponentiation: FORTRAN 77, PL/I and SNOBOL process coincident exponentiations from

---

‡ The other structures can be reduced to this form by introducing new variables.
† However, this cannot be ascertained at compile time, because *(A + B) + C* and *A + (B + C)* give difference results for floating point operands when *A* is very much greater than *B* and *C*.

right to left and thus come closer to the normal interpretation of a^{b^c}. FOR-TRAN 66 and ADA do not permit several exponentiations to coincide without the use of brackets.

Most languages give the unary plus and minus sign the same priority as the corresponding binary operators. PL/I, BASIC, ALGOL 68 and EUCLID (which incorporates only the unary minus) allocate the highest priority to the unary operators; ADA places them between the additive and multiplicative operators.† Whereas mathematical use of arithmetic formulae has a unifying effect, this is not so pronounced with the other operators. In general, arithmetic operators may be said to have a higher priority than the relational ones, which in their turn are placed higher than the Boolean operators.

A uniform priority level is normally allocated to the relational operators. Several relational operators can coincide only if uniform equality and inequality signs exist for all modes (including logical value mode).‡ For example, if the question is whether y is between x and z, but the size relationship between x and z is not known, then the following expression results:

$$IF\, x \leqslant y = y \leqslant z\ THEN\ ...$$

whereby the equality sign compares two Boolean operands with each other. ALGOL 60 introduces its own Boolean operator $EQUIV$ for the equality test on logical values, FORTRAN forbids it, PASCAL and ADA require the use of brackets. ALGOL 68 gives the equality and inequality signs lower priority than the other relational operators.

Negation usually has the highest priority amongst the Boolean operators. Conjunction comes next, followed by disjunction. ADA gives these two equal rank and puts negation on a level with the unary arithmetic operators. PASCAL gives the arithmetic operators no general priority over the Boolean ones but arranges them in the hierarchy existing at that point: conjunction is combined with the multiplicative, disjunction with the additive operators.

There are two final points for consideration: (1) The rules for operator priority establish only the sequence in which the operations are carried out, and not whether the left or right operand is the first to be evaluated. If function references with side effects appear in the operands, the results are very different. (2) On the other hand, most programming languages establish the operation sequence in more detail than the algorithm demands and the modern hardware possibilities require. The expression $A * B + C * D$, where the sequence of both multiplications is of no consequence provided that no side effects are possible, can be taken as an example.

9.2 Concatenation of statements

The simplest way of combining statements to form more extensive structures is concatenation. Languages such as FORTRAN, SNOBOL, or BASIC enter the

---

† The difference between specifications only affects the end result if coincident exponentiation is involved.

‡ This also applies to the case of implicit mode adjustment from logical values to arithmetic ones (PL/I).

individual statements on separate lines under each other, and thus in BASIC programs, the line numbers determine the sequence. Conversely, the format-free languages which are not line oriented require a separating character with which the end of one statement and the beginning of the next can be clearly indicated. The semicolon is the symbol most often used.

Languages of the ALGOL family as far as PASCAL consider the semicolon to be a separating character between statements. This means that there is no semicolon after the last statement in a sequence. Conversely, ADA and PL/I regard the semicolon as the termination character of a statement so that each statement ends with it. (PL/I separates the *DO* specification from the *DO* range by a semicolon.) ALGOL 68 uses a semicolon as a termination character only if it needs to be shown that the statements must be carried out one after the other in the sequence in which they are written down. If the sequence is irrelevant, a comma is used. Note that ALGOL 68 also regards the *EXIT* symbol as a termination character, but its actual meaning is the termination of the processed statement sequence.

9.3 Branching

Language constructs which allow branching but contain no corresponding junction are regarded with a certain scepticism by those involved in modern programming technology. This mistrust is based not so much on the fact that the constructs themselves are poor but rather that they have a greater tendency than others to lead to a program style which is not easy to grasp. The following belong to this group: (1) unconditional and conditional *GO TO* statements which cause the program to be continued at an explicitly indicated label; (2) *GO TO* statements in which the transfer target is selected from an array of possible transfer targets, using an index; (3) *GO TO* statements in which the transfer target is the value of a label variable and which correspond to indirect *GO TO* statements at machine level; (4) *GO TO* statements which are activated by the occurrence of a condition (exception handling).†

The *GO TO* statement is the simplest way of carrying out control flow at machine level and hence it can be found in almost all high-level programming languages. One exception is BLISS which showed early on that the explicit *GO TO* statement can be omitted if flexible control structures are available and other exceptions are languages which advocate a formal program verification, e.g. EUCLID.

One condition for the *GO TO* statement is that the statements to which control can be transferred must be clearly characterized by having a label in front of them. In BASIC programs, statements are characterized by an ascending order of line numbers; the transfer target is thus specified by giving the corresponding line number.‡ FORTRAN and PASCAL use arbitrarily selected natural numbers which do not necessarily ascend monotonically and which can have up to four or five digits. In FORTRAN, the label must be in the first five

---

† This is dealt with in chapter 10.
‡ Each time lines are renumbered, however, errors may be generated.

columns of the statement line; in PASCAL it is terminated by a colon and, in contrast to other languages, is declared as *LABEL* at the beginning of the block. Most languages prefer to use identifiers as labels (natural numbers are also allowed in ALGOL 60), and although these are not declared at the beginning of the block, they are covered by the normal validity range specifications. Labels are usually separated from the following statement by a colon; ADA encloses them in brackets ⟨⟨...⟩⟩. In COBOL programs, control can only be transferred to paragraphs; the relevant paragraph identifier functions as a label. SNOBOL represents a more pathological case: in labelled statements, the label begins in the first column, and in unlabelled ones, the first column is empty.

The predominant form of the *GO TO* statement is as follows:

GOTO transfertarget

where *transfertarget* can be a label, a component of a given fixed label array (switch), or a simple or subscripted variable name to which different labels can be assigned during the program run. A label array is a one-dimensional array, the components of which are labels. The *SWITCH* construction in ALGOL 60 is an example of this:

SWITCH switch : = label1, label2, ..., label ‡.

in which the component values are specified in the declaration. The corresponding *GO TO* statement is then

GOTO switch [subscript]

The subscript can be any arithmetic expression which results in a natural number not greater than the number of labels in the declaration. The *COMPUTED-GOTO* construction in FORTRAN is another example, but here the components are specified in the statement itself:

GOTO (label1, label2, ..., label), subscript †

Label variables are declared in FORTRAN as *INTEGER* and in PL/I as *LABEL*. A specific label can be assigned to them by means of a value assignment. Whereas PL/I uses the normal value assignment for this, FORTRAN has its own for labels:

ASSIGN label TO variable

A subsequent statement

GOTO variable

then causes a transfer to the label which was last assigned. FORTRAN 66 specifies (and FORTRAN 77 allows) that a list of possible transfer targets should be added to the *GO TO* statement:

GOTO variable,(label1, label2, ..., label)

---

‡ Apart from labels, label array components and conditional expressions may appear.
† The comma after the closing bracket is optional in FORTRAN 77.

Conditional *GO TO* statements are generally formed by the occurrence of a *GO TO* statement in one of the alternatives of a conditional statement. The arithmetic branch in FORTRAN

IF (arithmetic expression) label1, label2, label3

is an exception. Control is transferred to the first label if evaluation of the expression gives a negative result, to the second if the result is zero, and to the third if it is positive.

The clarity of *GO TO* statements depends very much on where the control is allowed to be transferred. Languages with only a little program structure simply forbid transfer into loops. (FORTRAN 66 is an exception: in this case, transfer may be into a loop if there has been a transfer out of it prior to this operation.) Over and above this, languages with block structure forbid transfer into a block. The more modern languages forbid transfer into all control structures and also between different alternatives of case discrimination.

9.4 Control structures in SNOBOL

SNOBOL incorporates a very convenient implicit loop which is given by scanning patterns.† Apart from this, SNOBOL has only very rudimentary control structures: transfer targets can be attached to each statement in order to determine the next statement to be executed:

statement	*:(label)*
statement	*:S(label)*
statement	*:F(label)*
statement	*:S(label1)F(label2)*

An *S* or an *F* in front of the bracketed transfer target means that control is to be transferred to this label if the statement was completed with *success* or with *failure*. Hence, the construction relates to the fact that the typical SNOBOL statements are concerned with scanning a given character string for a specific pattern. Successful termination of a statement thus means that the pattern (or one of its alternatives) has been found.

---

† See section 7.7.

10

Structured sequential control flow

Differences in the way the various programming languages formulate control structures are apparent at first glance. Structures can be classified according to whether or not they satisfy the requirement, which is essential to program clarity, to possess only one entry and one exit point. The normal cycle structures belong here, but the branch structures are only accepted if they meet up again. This is so in the modern *CASE* statements, but it does not cover the branching statements described in the previous chapter.

As the control structures in complex algorithms occur of necessity in a nested form, the question must be whether the formulation directly allows a unique bracketing, or whether the range of the control structure must be limited by auxiliary constructs. The *BEGIN-END* bracketing of ALGOL 60 which is always required when more than one statement belongs to the control range, or the use of statement numbers in FORTRAN *DO* loops are examples of this type of auxiliary constructs. For the sake of clarity, the trend is towards language constructs with a delimiting form, in which a direct conclusion to the construct is provided by a terminating symbol. In ALGOL 68, this is done by a rather refined form of symbol reversion (*IF . . . FI, DO . . . OD*) and in the newer languages different *END* symbols take the role (*IF . . . ENDIF, LOOP . . . ENDLOOP*). The PL/I solution of requiring the bracketing *BEGIN...END* for *IF*, and being satisfied with *END* for *DO* is not a very good one; apart from anything else, the facility of being able to contract several *END*s into one impedes automatic error recognition.

10.1 Case discrimination

Case discrimination provides a formulation where just one action from several alternatives is selected and carried out. Irrespective of which alternative is chosen, the program run is then continued at the statement following the case

a) Two-sided case discrimination

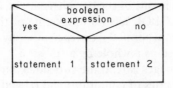

b) Multi-sided case discrimination with sequential evaluation

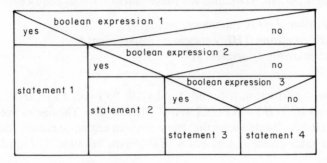

c) Multi-sided case discrimination with single evaluation

		criterion	
= value 1	= value 2	= value 3	= value 4
statement 1	statement 2	statement 3	statement 4

Fig. 10.1   Case discrimination.

discrimination.† The decision as to which alternative is to be carried out may be made (1) as a function of the value of a Boolean expression, or (2) based on a match between a criterion and one of the alternative values. The first case leads to two-sided alternatives as described by the classical *IF-THEN-ELSE* construct and the second to *CASE* constructs (Fig. 10.1). However, the definition is not a very sharp one and the *CASE* statement can be implemented by a nesting of *IF-THEN-ELSE*.

The classical form of one- or two-sided alternatives is the conditional statement in ALGOL 60:

IF condition THEN statement1 ELSE [statement2]

in which the bracketed part is optional.‡ It occurs in the same form in PASCAL and PL/I (with an additional semicolon before the *ELSE* in the latter case) and in a similar form in COBOL:

---

† As long as the alternatives given contain no jump instructions.
‡ See section 2.2.

IF condition; statement1 [ELSE statement2] .

If several statements are carried out in one of the two alternatives, a *BEGIN ... END* bracketing is necessary. As COBOL has nó bracketing of this type, the statements within the alternatives are separated from each other by a semicolon and case discrimination is terminated as a whole by a full stop.‡

LISP and the more modern languages extend the two-sided alternative to a multi-sided one. This consists of a series of conditions and related statements; the statement belonging to the first condition which adopts the value *true* is the one carried out. In ADA, this language construct is as follows:

IF condition THEN statement__sequence
{ELSIF condition THEN statement__sequence} *
[ELSE statement__sequence]
END IF

The same construction is found in ALGOL 68 (with *ELIF* and *FI* instead of *ELSIF* and *END IF*) and FORTRAN 77 (*ELSE IF*). The line oriented notation of FORTRAN also demands that the statement sequence always starts on a new line. The same construction, but with different notation, is found in LISP:

(COND
        {(condition statement)} *
        [(T   statement)]
)

The *ELSE* part is replaced here by the condition *T* (*true*).

In many cases, sequential evaluation of conditions is not necessary as the alternative can be selected at the beginning. One typical example is the processing of input data which can be interpreted in many ways, where the first input column specifies the processing mode. In ALGOL 68, the alternative is selected by an arithmetic expression,⁻which must give an integer value:

CASE expression IN
        statement {,statement} *
        [OUT statement]
ESAC

If evaluation of the expression gives a value between 1 and the specified number of statements, then the statement which is noted at the corresponding position is the one carried out. Should the value fall outside this range, then the (optional) statement after *OUT* is performed. The programmer must ensure a very disciplined textual arrangement if legibility is to be preserved.

Obligatory coding of possible alternatives by integers is avoided in PASCAL and ADA, and values of an arbitrary discrete type are allowed.† Those constants for which an alternative is to be performed must be explicitly specified in front of each alternative:

---

‡ This restricts the arbitrary nesting. The same applies for the Boolean *IF* in FORTRAN.
† The decision tables for which only pre-compilers are available as yet, present an even greater range of possibilities.

CASE expression OF
    { *WHEN value* = > *statement__sequence*} *
    [*WHEN OTHERS* = > *statement__sequence*]
END CASE

A list of several values can be specified instead of just one when the same statement sequence is to be performed. A range of values may also be specified in ADA.

10.2 Special aspects of case discrimination

The discussion of Boolean operators referred to the fact that the value of a compound condition is often determined after one of its parts has been evaluated. Most compilers use this property to generate a faster program. This allows the programmer to use incorrect formulations, for example:

IF i ≠ 0 AND a/i > 1 THEN statement

In this condition, the second operand will not be evaluated unless the first gives the value *true*. ALGOL 60 and ALGOL 68 make the following conditional expression construction available:

IF (IF i ≠ 0 THEN a/i > 1 ELSE FALSE) THEN statement

The 'short-circuit control forms' of ADA represents a clearer notation:

IF i /= Ø AND THEN a/i > 1 THEN statement

There is also an *OR ELSE*.

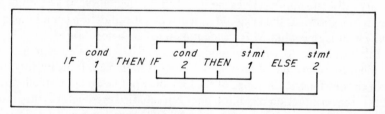

Fig. 10.2 Potential ambiguity when mixing one- and two-sided alternatives.

When one- and two-sided conditional statements are mixed, a syntactic ambiguity occurs when the *IF* statement is not terminated by a special symbol (*FI, END IF*) or the language involves other measures (see Fig. 10.2). It is not clear whether *stmt 2* should be performed when *cond1* is not satisfied (lower interpretation) or when *cond1* is satisfied but not *cond2* (upper interpretation). PASCAL chooses the second alternative. An *ELSE* always corresponds to 'he last *THEN*. ALGOL 60 rules out the construction and requires a conditional *THEN* part to be enclosed in *BEGIN* and *END*. PL/I regards the first part of a conditional statement, that is,

IF cond THEN stmt

as an independent statement; if the *ELSE* part is added inside the nest (upper interpretation), then this embraces two statements and must therefore be bracketed.

Finally, some languages allow case discriminations which are not based on relations between objects of the same (or comparable) mode, but on the question as to whether the object is of a specific mode. LISP permits the enquiry as to whether the object is an atom or not. ADA can ask whether an object of a given mode conforms to the restrictions placed on a sub-mode, for example:

$x + y$ IN small_number

In ALGOL 68, union modes can be considered. If an object is declared by *UNION (mode1, mode2)*, then the actual mode can be questioned within the framework of a conformity clause:

CASE object IN
(mode1:) statement1,
(mode2:) statement2
ESAC †

10.3 *FOR* statements (loops)

Loop structures are used when a statement sequence (*DO* range or *FOR* range) is to be repeated. They can be classified in various ways: (1) The number of passes through the loop may be fixed before repetition is begun or it may not be fixed at this point. (2) The inquiry as to whether the loop process is finished may be made at the beginning or at the end of each pass.§

If the number of loop passes is fixed at the beginning of loop processing, then the *DO* specification must incorporate a number specification. In general, the specification of an interval of integers is sufficient, but in many cases, the use of arbitrary, discrete modes gives better program legibility. If the number of passes is not known at the beginning, then a *DO* specification containing a condition which is re-evaluated for each pass must be incorporated.

If the inquiry as to whether loop processing is terminated is made at the beginning, this is evaluated even before the first loop pass. It means that, under certain circumstances, the range of the loop may not be executed at all, and this applies if the termination condition has been satisfied even before entry into the loop. If the inquiry occurs at the end, the *DO* range is executed at least once even if the termination condition was previously satisfied. Many practical problems can be much more safely formulated if the inquiry is at the beginning, because the number of loop passes is frequently given by a variable (e.g. list length) and the program will still operate correctly even if this is 0. There are just a few examples, however, in which the termination condition cannot be correctly evaluated before the first loop pass, e.g. mathematical iteration processes where a new value for calculation is to be compared with a previous one. As most languages have the test at the beginning only, the programmer must make use of additional statements as well.‡

---

† Only modes which occur in the *UNION* declaration can be used.
§ The inquiry inside the FOR range certainly makes sense basically, but it is not used in current languages.
‡ For example, a value assignment which ensures that the condition gives the value *false* the first time.

ALGOL 60	*FOR variable : = startvalue STEP stepsize UNTIL endvalue* *DO for range*
ALGOL 68	*FOR variable FROM startvalue [BY stepsize] TO endvalue* *DO for__ range OD*
PL/I	*DO variable = startvalue TO endvalue [BY stepsize];* *for__ range* *END;*
PASCAL	*FOR variable : = startvalue TO endvalue* *DO for__ range;*
ADA	*FOR variable IN discrete__ interval* *LOOP for__ range END LOOP;*
FORTRAN	*DO label variable = startvalue, endvalue [, stepsize]* *for range__ without__ last__ statement* *label last__ statement*
BASIC	*FOR variable = startvalue TO endvalue [STEP stepsize]* *for__ range* *NEXT variable*
COBOL	*PERFORM for__ rangeidentification* *VARYING variable FROM startvalue BY stepsize* *UNTIL condition.* †

Fig. 10.3 Loop statements with counting loop control. If the variable runs backwards, *TO* is replaced by *DOWNTO* in PASCAL and *IN* by *INREVERSE* in ADA.

In the very widely used counting loop specifications, repetitions are controlled by a loop variable (Fig. 10.3): an initial value is assigned to this and a check is made before each loop pass to see whether its value has exceeded or, in the case of negative increments, fallen below the terminating value. After each loop pass, the value of the loop variable is altered by that of the increment. Differences in form are not essential except for those between the variable components allowed.

In general, integer loop variables are accepted. Over and above this, ALGOL 60, FORTRAN 77 and BASIC permit real value variables, and FORTRAN 77 allows double precision ones. This causes problems due to the rounding error‡ which cannot be ruled out with floating point calculations. ADA allows the loop variable to pass through an arbitrary interval of a discrete mode, for example:

FOR clothescolour IN red .. blue LOOP ... END LOOP

This interval must be traversed without gaps; an increment is not given explicitly. Thus, for systematic reasons, even integer control intervals are restricted to increments $+1$ and -1. However, other increments can be achieved by declaring an integer sub-mode by a suitable *DELTA* and then using an interval from this mode.§ Similarly, PASCAL only incorporates the increments $+1$ and -1. In languages allowing arbitrary increments, the $+1$ can often be omitted. FORTRAN 66 and COBOL use only positive increments. Moreover, FORTRAN 66 does not permit the terminating value to be less than the initial one. Hence, it does not matter whether the termination condition is checked at

† COBOL requires an end condition instead of a final value.
‡ See section 6.3.
§ See section 4.3.

the beginning or the end of the pass through the loop. As the relation between terminating and initial value cannot be checked at translation time, 'dirty tricks' programmers can make use of the position of the inquiry in 'their' compiler, and this leads to program incompatibility when transferred to FORTRAN 77.

ALGOL family and PL/I languages use arbitrary expressions for determining initial, terminating and increment values. The question here is whether these expressions have to be re-evaluated for each pass or evaluated only once before entering the loop. PL/I and ALGOL 68 opt for the latter. The definition of ALGOL 60 is not clear on this point. Further details are provided by Knuth (1967).

The second group of loops, in which the number of passes cannot be fixed before entry, is handled much more uniformly in the different programming languages by the *WHILE* loop:

WHILE condition LOOP range END LOOP

PASCAL, ADA, and all the more recent languages incorporate corresponding structures. The condition is re-evaluated before each pass and the loop range is only repeated when the condition is satisfied further. Obviously this form of loop involves the danger of becoming an infinite loop: the variables included in the condition must be modified in the loop range in such a way that at some point in time the condition is no longer fulfilled. EUCLID makes this danger clear by leaving out the condition:

LOOP range END LOOP

and the loop range cannot be abandoned without special statements. BLISS and PASCAL allow the inquiry to be deferred until the end of the pass through the loop:

REPEAT range UNTIL condition

ALGOL 68 and PL/I allow a combination of the *WHILE* construct with the counting loop control:

FOR loopvariable FROM startvalue BY stepsize TO endvalue
                       WHILE condition
DO range OD

This enables the numerically controlled loop to be terminated prematurely. ALGOL 60 combines the *WHILE* construct with the loop variable:

FOR loopvariable : = expression WHILE condition
DO range

If *loopvariable + increment* is chosen as the expression then the above ALGOL 68 loop is made. However, manipulation of this ALGOL 60 variant is often tiresome.

10.4 Determination and abandonment of the loop range

The loop range, i.e. the statement sequence for repetition, is determined differently by the individual programming languages. As most programming languages allow nesting of loops, the range must be delimited. Languages influenced by ALGOL use either the symbol pair *BEGIN ... END* (ALGOL 60, PASCAL), which also occurs in another context, as a statement delimiter, or special symbol pairs which are used specifically in loop ranges, e.g. *DO ... OD* (ALGOL 68) or *LOOP ... END LOOP* (ADA). PL/I, FORTRAN, and BASIC mark only the end of the range. PL/I uses *END* for this and BASIC uses *NEXT* together with the loop variable. FORTRAN marks the last statement belonging to the loop range by a statement number which is named in the loop specification and achieves a delimiting effect.

If the ends of several nested loop ranges coincide, then only a common end label can be used for all ranges in PL/I and FORTRAN. This convenient way of writing a program does not lend itself to being readily changed. When processing multi-dimensional arrays in particular, it often happens that not only the ends of loop ranges coincide but also the beginnings: the computation in the range is the same for the whole array without the need for additional statements when a row or column change occurs. In COBOL programs, the corresponding loop specifications can be combined to form a single one:

VARYING i ... AFTER j ...

in which the dots indicate the description of the beginning, the end, and the increments.

Basically, a loop is abandoned when the termination criterion specified by the loop specification occurs, e.g. when a *WHILE* condition is no longer fulfilled, or when the terminating value of a counting loop is exceeded. (In this context, it should be pointed out that many languages are based on the fact that the loop variable is then undefined and does not keep the last value in force in the loop range.) This termination always occurs between two passes through the range. If the loop is to be terminated at an arbitrary place in the range,† then the classical languages provide only the general branch instruction, with which a jump can be made to any target statement. To avoid this general branch instruction, the newer languages offer special branch instructions by which only disciplined jumps are allowed: loop processing is terminated and the program run continued with the statement following the loop. For example, ADA formulates this as follows:

EXIT WHEN condition

The condition part is missing in an unconditional exit. Even several nested statements can be abandoned at a stroke by specifying a suitable label. The first language to provide these statements was BLISS; it incorporates this type of termination statement for all compound statements and not just the loop. In COBOL, the termination effect is achieved by means of the statement *NEXT SENTENCE*, as long as the loop range consists of one sentence only.

The termination statements just discussed also ensure that the program run

---

† The literature sometimes refers to *(n + 1/2)* loops because after *n* passes a further execution of the loop has still been only partly processed.

continues after the loop. Premature termination of a loop is often related to the occurrence of a certain event, e.g. the discovery of a required value in a list. Specific actions related to this event may then be carried out. Zahn (1974) has proposed a very flexible language construct for this purpose (Fig. 10.4). If one of the named conditions occurs, loop processing is terminated, and the statement sequence assigned to this condition is performed. A similar language element has been incorporated into MODULA by Wirth (1977a). The other control structures considered can be regarded as special cases of Zahn's loop.

> *LOOP UNTIL cond1 OR ... OR condn:*
> *statement__ sequence;*
>
> *REPEAT;*
>
> *THEN cond1 = > statement__ sequence;*
>   ...
>   *condn = > statement__ sequence;*
> *FI*

Fig. 10.4   Zahn's loop.

10.5 Special aspects of loops

The only language which does not append the loop range directly to the loop specification is COBOL. In this case, the fact that COBOL programs are divided into paragraphs which bear an identification is important. This identification, or that of the first and the last paragraphs when several make up the loop range, is given in the loop specification:

PERFORM par1 THRU par2 VARYING subscript ...

In FORTRAN 66, one characteristic which does not help program legibility is the extended loop range. If the range which is enclosed by the loop specification and its last statement is left by means of a jump, another jump can lead back into the same range; the statements passing between the two jumps belong to the loop range!

SNOBOL, LISP and APL have no explicit loops. In LISP, loops have to be simulated by recursive procedure calls. In SNOBOL and APL, loops can be constructed only by jump statements; however, both languages contain implicit loops for a large number of their typical tasks: SNOBOL uses pattern set searches and APL compound operators for array processing. The SEARCH statements in COBOL and the set-theoretic operations in SETL in which implicit loops are also involved should be mentioned in this context.

Finally, there is the concatenation of various loop specifications for the same control variable, as used by ALGOL 60 and PL/I:

FOR i := 1 STEP 1 UNTIL j − 1, j + 1 STEP 1 UNTIL n DO ...

This compound loop specification skips the case $i = j$, for example, omitting the diagonals of a matrix.

10.6 Exception handling

When algorithms are performed, special cases can occur which make it impossible to proceed with the next statement and which require exception handling. Division by a number close to *0* which produces an arithmetic overflow immediately springs to mind. The inevitable program termination causes no damage in many applications,† but the picture is somewhat different for cases such as process control systems, where the exceptions are often those points to which the program has to respond especially quickly. Even when many software processes run in parallel in a computer system, each must have the chance to break off its pre-planned algorithmic statement sequence when certain events are signalled from another process. It is becoming increasingly accepted, and rightly so, that all these interruptions to a normal program run must and can be described in a uniform manner.

Languages such as ALGOL 60 and FORTRAN 66, which were designed exclusively for formulation of algorithms, do not incorporate any language construct for exception handling. As long as the exception occurs within the algorithm (arithmetic error, overflow of storage areas provided, etc.) the programmer can intercept it by regular and time consuming inquiry of relevant variables. Language constructs for exception handling remove this burden from the programmer; they allow him to specify measures to be carried out when an exception occurs. Two different concepts have emerged. The first regards exception handling as an insertion into the normal program run, which is subsequently continued. The second considers it to be a reason for terminating the program run at least at the level of the program unit just processed (procedure, block).

If exception handling is regarded as a normal progamming technique and not necessarily as an error, then when the exception occurs, a special program unit is called and the normal sequence is resumed after that has been executed. This means, in particular, that the data in the interrupted program section are preserved. If an error is involved, then the exception handling must remove the cause, or contain instructions for ending the program unit (e.g. procedure return). Goodenough (1975) and Parnas and Wurges (1976) have made some suitable proposals to deal with these eventualities.

In the second case, the interrupted program run is not continued after exception handling, but the statement sequence which is called must itself decide how to continue: (1) it may start the interrupted program unit again with modified data, (2) it may continue with the calling program unit (calling procedure, surrounding block) as if nothing had happened, and (3) it may also put exception handling in the calling program unit into operation too. Horning *et al.* (1974) and Randell (1975) have made suitable suggestions for solving the problem.

Exception handling in PL/I is very complex (Noble, 1969) and hence only a few points are covered here. One or more excpetion conditions can be specified in a program unit in the form

ON condition [*SNAP*] *statement*

---

† There is no alternative for languages with no explicit exception handling.

(Similar exception conditions are found in COBOL.) This means that when the specified condition occurs, the assigned statement is carried out. A compound statement, as well as a simple one, is possible, for example:

ON ENDFILE GOTO print;
ON ZERODIVIDE CALL columnchange;
ON SUBSCRIPTRANGE BEGIN ; ... ; END;

If the word symbol *SYSTEM* is given instead of a statement, then standard measures are employed; this also happens when there is no *ON* specification provided. (The optional word symbol *SNAP* ensures in addition that a snapshot of the program process is printed.)

PL/I specifies three groups of conditions: (1) those which are always operational, (2) those which can be turned off by prefixes, and (3) those which must be turned on by prefixes. The first group, which always cause a reaction, incorporates the test for reading beyond the end of a file (standard handling: program termination), for printing further at the end of a page (standard handling: beginning of a new page), or bringing more elements than provided by the declaration into an area in list processing. The second group of exception conditions, which are normally turned on, contains predominantly the arithmetic errors: overflow, underflow, zero division. The third group of exception conditions, which must be explicitly turned on, covers such things as the occurrence of subscripts which are outside the subscript range.

Turning on and off (groups 2 and 3 above) is done by condition prefixes which can be written in front of simple statements, compound statements, or procedures. The additional *NO* acts as a turn-off:

ON SUBSCRIPTRANGE GOTO m;
(NOFIXEDOVERFLOW, SUBSCRIPTRANGE):
BEGIN; ... ;END;

This means that there is no reaction to the overflow of fixed point numbers in the indicated block, and when the subscript range of an array is violated a jump is made to label *m*.

ADA belongs to the second language group mentioned, i.e. when an exception arises, the normal statement sequence is terminated and exception handling is performed instead. There is no continuation of the terminated program unit. The measures to be taken are appended at the end of a block, subprogram, or module (Fig. 10.5).

The exception conditions are labelled with identifiers and declared in the normal way:

condition : EXCEPTION

As ADA uses not only predefined exception conditions but also those newly defined in the program, a statement to raise them is necessary:

RAISE condition

Like all declarations, those attached to exception conditions in ADA programs are governed by block structure. Several consequences which can only be brief-

```
BEGIN
        normal__ statement__ sequence;
EXCEPTION
        WHEN condition__ list__ 1 = > statement__ 1;
        WHEN condition__ list__ 2 = > statement__ 2;
        . . .
        WHEN OTHERS = > statement;
END
```

Fig. 10.5   Structure of an ADA block with exception handling.

```
PROCEDURE p IS
        error: EXCEPTION;
        PROCEDURE q IS
        BEGIN r;
        -- possibility (2) for the apearance of the ex-
        -- ception;
        EXCEPTION WHEN error = > -- handling e2;
        END q;
        PROCEDURE r IS
        BEGIN -- possibility (3) for the appearance of the ex-
                        ception;
        END r;
BEGIN -- possibility (1) for the appearance of the exception;
        q; r;
EXCEPTION WHEN error = > -- handling e1;
END p
```

Fig. 10.6   Dynamic assignment of exception handling in ADA.

ly mentioned here result from this. If a program unit contains no local exception handling for a raised condition, then the processing of this program unit is terminated, and the exception condition is passed to the calling program unit. (Exception handling is not specified if the condition does not appear in any of the condition lists and there is no *OTHERS* alternative offered.) The calling program unit, which must now handle the exception, is the surrounding block in the case of blocks and the calling procedure in the case of procedures. At this point, either an exception handling is provided or the condition is handed on further.

In view of the dynamic call hierarchy in subprograms, a condition occurring at a certain place can cause several different effects: Ichbiah *et al.* (1979) give several examples, one of which is given in a slightly modified version below (Fig. 10.6):

(1) The exception condition *error* occurs in the body of outermost procedure *p*. The exception handling *e1* available in this procedure is performed.

(2) *Error* occurs in the body of procedure *q*. Handling *e2* is performed.

(3) *Error* occurs in the body of *r* which provides no special handling for this exception. One might expect that *e1* in the statically surrounding procedure would be executed, but the condition is passed to the calling procedure: either to *q* (handling via *e2*) or to *p* (*e1* is performed).

11

Procedures

Program statements are usually performed in the sequence written by the programmer and the control structures already discussed are then used to establish any variations of this sequence. Just as, in the section on data, we switched over from simple objects to compound ones which could then occur as a unit in specific statements, several statements can also be incorporated to form a unit which outwardly acts as a single new statement. The effect can be characterized by the 'black-box philosophy' concept; the programmer can use this new statement (procedure call) as a black box wherever he requires an algorithm with specific properties, without having to be involved in its implementation details.†

Procedures were used in the first instance to overcome the need for repeatedly writing statement sequences which occurred many times in a program. The saving of storage space and writing time were also taken into consideration. It was very quickly realized that, once written, such algorithms could be used in other programs. This new aspect demanded a high degree of flexibility, which was achieved by using parameters. The idea of using procedures to assist in program structuring has become highly significant with the need to transfer large scale programs between systems. This structuring can lead either to a hierarchical relationship between procedures in which one is instructed by the other to process a subtask fully and report the result (subroutine), or to an evenly balanced collaboration (coroutines, parallel processes).

11.1 Control flow in subroutines

A subroutine call means that the processing of statements from the calling program is temporarily interrupted and a jump is made to the beginning of the

---

† The macro-instructions, which are used mostly in assembler languages, have a similar but somewhat more static effect.

subroutine. If the statment sequence in a subroutine is terminated, a jump is made back to the point in the calling program from which the call was made and the flow of control which was broken off is continued at the next statement. Termination of the subroutine is here regarded as its logical end; this may be the execution of the textually last statement but could also be a return jump executed at an earlier point in the subroutine. Hence, Fig. 11.1 should be regarded as a dynamic representation.

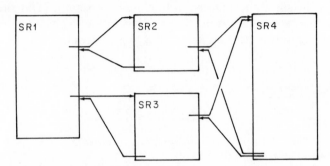

Fig. 11.1   Mutual call of subroutines.

As the subroutine can be called from various points in the main program,† the normal jump statement is not adequate for programming the return: the transfer target is dependent on the location of the subroutine call. Hence a pair of jump statements which will set up this connection is required: (1) The subroutine call statement (CALL) must not only perform the jump to the beginning of the subroutine but must also note the location of the calling program, so that continuation can be made from there at a later stage (return address). (2) The return statement (RETURN) contains no explicit target information but relates to the entry made at the time of the corresponding subroutine call. Machine instructions are usually available for both.

The nested call, in which subroutines in their turn can call other subroutines, involves no new concepts for the programmer to deal with, as the relationship between the calling and the called program does not change. However, a new feature is introduced when the called program is identical to the calling one (direct recursion) or such an identity is established over several levels of subroutine nesting (indirect recursion). In LISP, recursion is a fundamental concept, but FORTRAN, COBOL, and BASIC do not allow recursive subroutines. The reason for this is that recursive subroutines require a dynamic storage administration.

The fact that some widely-used languages forbid recursion can be used as a starting point for discussing the usefulness of this concept. Programming textbooks often clarify it by means of very simple examples which can also be clearly formulated by loops, e.g. the greatest common division. However, there are algorithms which can be clearly and directly formulated by recursion, whereas

---

† For simplicity, the calling program is called the main program, even when it is itself a subroutine.

an equivalent iterative formulation is rather confused. Syntax analysis in compilers provides an example which is of practical use (Jensen and Wirth 1978). The Hanoi towers problem is a good visual example (Fig. 11.2): the problem involved is how to transport a pyramid composed of individual stones from position A to position B. Position C is available as an interim storage point. The stones must be moved individually and at no point should the bigger ones be on top of the smaller ones. The recursive solution is based on the simple concept that the bottom stone of a tower of height n can be placed in the target position if a tower of height $n-1$ is placed in the interim position. (This situation is outlined by the dashed lines in the figure). Hence case n is based on case $n-1$ and the task is resolved because $n = 1$ or $n = 0$ is trivial.

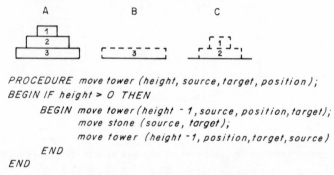

```
PROCEDURE move tower (height, source, target, position);
BEGIN IF height > 0 THEN
       BEGIN move tower (height - 1, source, position, target);
             move stone (source, target);
             move tower (height - 1, position, target, source)
       END
END
```

Fig. 11.2   PASCAL—version of the 'Hanoi towers' concept.

11.2 Form of procedure and procedure call

Apart from the standard procedures which are predefined and may arbitrarily be used by the programmer as required, all procedures must be declared. Procedures can be looked at from two angles: the location and validity range of the declaration, and the mode of usage.

Under the heading of mode of usage, procedures which are called as functions within expressions and are normally identified as function procedures are distinguished from those in which the call is an independent statement. This difference plays only a minor role when dealing with location and validity range of the declaration: FORTRAN and BASIC use function statements and these can occur within other program units. This represents a simplified form of procedure declaration for function procedures. A further distinction should be made to ascertain whether procedures are external and translated as independent units, or whether the declarations are subject to the normal validity range regulations (e.g. block structure). Note that all languages not using block structure or module structure treat all procedures as if they were external, conversely, languages with validity range nesting handle procedure declarations in the same way as the other declarations.† PL/I adopts a middle way in which both exter-

---

† If external procedures are used in block structured languages, then the heading must be repeated within the required validity range.

nal procedures (with global validity range) and declaration within the block structure are permitted. In ALGOL, procedure declaration can be mixed arbitrarily with other declarations. In PASCAL and its successors they must be noted immediately after the other declarations.‡

Procedure declaration involves a procedure heading and a procedure body. Whereas the procedure body describes the algorithm to be executed, the heading forms the syntactic interface between procedure call and body description. Its specifications are required firstly to provide a syntactically correct formulation for the procedure call, and secondly to check such things as parameter usage in the procedure body. The procedure heading is comprised of: (1) the procedure identifier, (2) the specification as to whether the procedure is called as a function or a statement, (3) the number, ordering, and identifiers of parameters, and (4) the parameter mode and, in the case of function procedures, the mode of the value returned as its result which must fit within the framework in which declarations are accepted in the language. In some languages, further specifications may occur. For example, in PL/I, recursive or reentrant procedures must be labelled as such. EUCLID allows the programmer to specify parameter values both before and after the procedure body has been performed (pre- and post-conditions).†

In general, the identifiers for procedure naming have the same form as those for any other objects. One exception to this is BASIC, in which the function procedure identifiers begin with *FN* followed by a letter. In extended BASIC systems, a digit, or a dollar sign in the case of text functions, can be added on; some systems allow arbitrary identifiers for external procedures. ALGOL 68 and some of the newer languages like ADA form another type of exception; any characters can be used for procedure names and hence new operators can be introduced.

The more programmers use procedures as an aid to program structuring, the greater is the number of procedure declarations contained in a program. This leads to long declaration parts which contain a syntactic specification (heading) together with relevant algorithmic detail. Only the procedure headings are important to the calling program and body details are not used. ADA allows all procedure headings and normal declarations to be summarized in a declaration part which is followed by a separate part containing the bodies.§ In the case of a module, a procedure heading can be made outwardly visible in this way.

The distinction already made between procedures which are called as functions within expressions and those called as statements also applies to procedure calls.

Function procedures are picked up as a whole in the mathematically well-known notation form

function__designation (list__of__actual__parameters)

---

‡ This avoids the situation which arises in Fig. 8.1, line 6.
† The fact that EUCLID syntax allocates these conditions to the procedure body is not wholly consistent.
§ In defining the procedure bodies, the headings belonging to them must be completely repeated, although this is actually unnecessary.

As long as the language permits any special characters as function designators, the infix notation is consistent;

first__parameter operator second__parameter

(APL uses this notation alone.) In ALGOL 68 programs, any new characters can be introduced as operators, whereas ADA only allows a redefinition of existing ones or their definition for newly introduced parameter modes.

Procedures are called both in the ALGOL family of languages and in SNOBOL using the same notation:

procedures__designation (list__of__actual__parameters)

Most other languages use the keyword *CALL* to identify statements which call procedures. In BASIC, this form is used for external procedures only, whereas internal procedures are picked up by *GOSUB* (with no possibility of parameter passing).

11.3 Parameters

The re-usability of a procedure, once defined, depends to a great extent on its flexibility. One special aspect of this is that the algorithm described by the procedure has the chance to be performed with different data. Hence, the procedure requires access to objects which are defined in the calling program. From a program methodology point of view, the possibility of access to global objects is dubious and is not in fact adequate for working with different objects. However, parameters are suitable: a formal parameter is used in the procedure in all places where such an access is required; it is an identifier to which no concrete object is assigned. It is in fact a dummy argument which must be replaced by a suitable actual parameter in calling the procedure. The actual parameter is an object which is present in the call environment; its declaration, or that of the operands in the case of expressions, must therefore be valid at the call point. (It makes no difference whether or not the procedure body falls into the validity range.)

When a procedure is called, the actual parameters used must be compatible with the formal parameter specification. As a general rule, the actual parameters must correspond to the formal ones both in number and ordering. The sequence determines which actual parameter is to be used for which formal one. However, the documentation value of a program can be increased by repeating the formal parameter identifiers explicitly in the procedure call. For instance, ADA accepts the following call:

m := meanvalue(table = t1, size = n, column = 2)

This version takes longer to write, but the parameter sequence is not important,† and the order of parameters can be exchanged at will. It would not be permitted in languages which only allow positional parameter association

---

† This notation means that some parameters can be omitted as long as their value is not required for a concrete procedure call or is defined in another way (default value).

```
     REAL PROCEDURE meanvalue (table, column, size);
         ·INTEGER column, size;
         REAL ARRAY table;
     BEGIN INTEGER line; REAL sum;
         sum : = 0.0;
         FOR line : = 1 STEP 1 UNTIL size DO
             sum : = sum + table[line, column];
         meanvalue : = sum/item
     END;
     Call example
         difference : = meanvalue(t1, 1, 100)
         – meanvalue(t1, 2, 100)
```

Fig. 11.3   Example of an ALGOL 60 procedure.

such as ALGOL 60, but rather

   $m := meanvalue(t1, 2, n)$

(based on Fig. 11.3) would be used instead.

As the formal parameter does not identify any concrete object, it needs no declaration. However, the compiler needs information on the type of objects which can be used for formal parameters, in order to translate the procedure body. This information can be given in a form identical or similar to a declaration. FORTRAN 66 and PL/I directly use declarations which are not removed from local declarations in the procedure body. In comparison, the ALGOL family of languages provide their own specifications which are taken from the procedure body, and differ from the declarations in that information relating to concrete objects is omitted (e.g. array subscript range). The specifications may be at two different points in the procedure body: (1) The mode of each parameter is given directly in the list of formal parameters, i.e. still in the corresponding brackets:

   PROCEDURE meanvalue = (REF [,] REAL table, INT column, INT size)
   REAL

This solution is typical of ALGOL 68 (Fig. 11.3), as well as of PASCAL and its successors;† it is a systematic way, as the parameters have to be named once only. (2) The parameter mode is given in an appendix to the list of formal parameters, but still before the beginning of the procedure body, and the local objects are declared in it. This solution is typical of ALGOL 60 and languages derived from it such as SIMULA. The statement functions of FORTRAN represent a special case. As they are written in single lines, parameters cannot be specified within the procedure at all; the task is taken over by the surrounding program provided that implicit declaration rules are not applied.

Most formal parameters are treated in the procedure body in the same way as the identifier of a simple variable. As the actual parameters are used at the corresponding points in the procedure body, only simple or subscripted variables, constants, or the result of numerical expressions are considered. In this case,

---

† Specification of a parameter as an array is also done at this point in BASIC.

the mode of the referenced object or result of the actual parameter must be compatible with formal parameter specification. All the important programming languages allow array identifiers as parameters too. The differences lie in whether the array bounds must be explicitly given in the specification or can be implicitly assumed (at run time at the earliest) from the array specification given by the actual parameter. This implicit passing is used by ALGOL 60 (in which the number of subscripts is not specified either), PL/I, and ALGOL 68. In comparison, FORTRAN 66 requires explicit information on array bounds, and this is either done by prescribing it as a constant value in the specification or making it a formal parameter itself.‡ The possibility of using procedure identifiers as parameters leads to problems when a syntactic check is made on the procedure body: ALGOL 60 specifies only the type of result *(mode PRO-CEDURE)* or the fact that it is a statement procedure *(PROCEDURE)*. The same applies to PASCAL, FORTRAN and PL/I. However, the latter accepts that more detailed information on the parameter mode in a formal procedure identification can be given by an *ENTRY* specification. ALGOL 68 actually requires this:

PROC integrate = (PROC(REAL) REAL function_to_be_integrated,
REAL from, to, precision) REAL:
BEGIN ... END

Only function procedures which have real valued arguments and a real value result can be used for the first formal parameter.

11.4 Parameter passing

Problem oriented programming languages incorporate various ways of replacing formal parameters by those actual ones given by the program call.

(1) The actual parameter may be evaluated (i.e. its value is calculated) at the time of the function call and this constant then replaces the formal parameter at all points where it is used in the procedure body (*call by value*). As only constants can be passed to the procedure, no value can be assigned to these parameters there.†

(2) The actual parameter replaces the formal parameter literally (*call by name*). Its value is not determined until the program run reaches a point in the procedure body where the parameter is used. If it occurs several times, it is evaluated several times, and this is time consuming. If the actual parameter is a variable or an expression, a new value may result from each calculation: this is especially the case if one of the operands has been changed in between. This technique often leads to complex possibilities.

(3) The address of the actual parameter is passed to the procedure in calling it (*call by reference*). If an expression formed by operations or functions is involved

---

‡ However, in FORTRAN, the array in a procedure can be used with a number of subscripts or bounds different from those in the calling program.

† In ALGOL 60, a variable which is not visible to the programmer replaces the formal parameter and has a value assigned to it. Hence it can be changed within the procedure without any visible change in the calling program.

```
INTEGER ARRAY a [1:10]; INTEGER i,x;
PROCEDURE f(p); INTEGER p;
BEGIN i := 2;
        a[1] := 12;
        x := p
END f;
a[1] := 10; a[2] := 11; i := 1;
f(a[i]);
```

Fig. 11.4 Program example for the various parameter mechanisms (ALGOL 60 notation).

rather than the name of a single or subscripted variable, this expression is evaluated and the result assigned to a dummy variable which is not visible to the programmer. This parameter passing mechanism means that the formal parameter can be handled within the procedure like a simple variable. The value can be changed and this change becomes visible in the calling program.

The example shown in Fig. 11.4, which is formulated using ALGOL 60 as a basis, shows that the various parameter passing mechanisms are not only a concern for the authors of the compiler but can be used to give different results.

At the end of the program run, x can have various values dependent on the parameter passing mechanism used: (1) At the time of the procedure call, the constant $10 (= a[1])$ is used for p; hence x has the value 10 at the end. (2) $a[i]$ is used in the text for p and not evaluated until the value assignment $x := p$ is reached. However, at this point in time, i will have been given a value of 2, so that x becomes the value $a[2]$, hence 11. (3) The address of the actual parameter $a[i]$ is substituted for p at procedure call time, that is $a[1]$. The value assignment $x := a[1]$ thus reacts to the above change in $a[1]$ but the change in i has no effect.

The mechanism to be used in a procedure can be determined (1) for the programming language in general, (2) by the programmer in the procedure declaration, or it can result (3) from the actual parameters used. One example of the last instance is given in note (2) to Fig. 11.5. In some of the newer languages, e.g. ADA, the *call-by-result* mechanism is included as a counterpart to the *call-by-value* one. The value is given back to the calling program, on return. If both mechanisms are combined for the same parameter, the effect matches the *call-by-reference*, as long as there is no chance of access to the actual parameter between the beginning and the end of procedure handling.†

The *call-by-name* mechanism not only leads to inefficient programs as a result of repeated evaluation, but also has a dangerous 'flexibility'. Knuth and Merner (1961) have proposed a general problem solver which is so versatile that it does in fact justify its name (Fig. 11.6). The first call forms the sum $a[1] + a[2] + \ldots + a[100]$; the second call allocates the value $a[i,j] = i+j$ to each component of a matrix $a[1:n, 1:m]$.

---

† This possibility exists when the actual parameter is common to two processes running in parallel, or one procedure, given as an actual parameter, can read or change the other parameter.

Language	Value	Reference	Name
ALGOL 60	VALUE	-	implicit
SIMULA	implicit	for certain modes	NAME
ALGOL 68[1]	mode	REF mode	-
COBOL	-	-	-
APL	implicit	-	-
BASIC	implicit for functions	implicit for external subroutines	-
PL/I[2]	-	implicit	-
FORTRAN[2]	-	implicit	-
PASCAL	implicit	VAR	-
LISP	-	-	implicit
SNOBOL[3]	implicit	-	-
ADA[4]	IN	-	-

Fig. 11.5   Parameter mechanisms in the individual languages.
1   An effect similar to the call-by-name can be achieved by PROC mode.
2   An invisible dummy variable is generated in the case of constants and expressions; the effect then matches the call-by-value.
3   The value-passing can be suppressed by the asterisk operator.
4   See text.

```
INTEGER PROCEDURE problemsolver
        (controlvariable, end, left, right);
        INTEGER controlvariable, end, left, right;
BEGIN
        FOR controlvariable := 1 STEP 1 UNTIL end
        DO left := right;
        problemsolver := 1;
END problemsolver;
s := Ø; i := problemsolver (i, 1ØØ,s,s+a[i]);
i := problemsolver (j,m,i,problemsolver(i,n,a[i,j],i+j))
```

Fig. 11.6   General problem solver according to Knuth and Merner (1961).

11.5 Some special aspects of procedures

There are two ways of communicating results to the calling program in procedure statements. Firstly, a new value can be assigned to parameters in the procedure body; this value assignment changes the actual variable used if no *call-by-value* is present. Secondly, an item which is global with respect to the procedure can be changed in the procedure body. In the case of function procedures, the older languages also permit this mechanism. However, it is generally recognized today, that this is bad programming style (*side effects*). The fact that function calls occur in expressions actually results from the function value being processed further. Changing parameters or global items can have unforeseen results: on the one hand, not all operands in Boolean expressions have to be evaluated before a result is obtained, and on the other, it is often better for program optimization if the sequence of operand evaluation is left open. Neither case makes clear whether the side effects have been carried out and at what point in time. ADA expressly forbids side effects.

In the case of arithmetic operators, it is often taken for granted that various operators (e.g. integer and real value addition) are given the same identification: the operand mode indicates which operation is actually intended. The validity ranges of user-declared procedures could overlap in the same way. However, the parameter mode must allow a clear identification to be made.†
Most programming languages use this technique of identifier overloading for standard functions only. For example, in FORTRAN 77, the identifier SQRT can also be used for double-precision and complex arguments. Languages which operate with user-defined modes are especially likely to increase their flexibility by using this overloading technique, because existing algorithms can be adopted for related modes. On the other hand, the fact that too liberal an overloading can lead to confusion should not be forgotten either. ALGOL 68 and ADA allow operator overloading and ADA accepts it for procedures too.

PL/I has introduced the possibility of declaring procedures with several entries. Similar structures are also found in PEARL and FORTRAN 77. The corresponding program positions are labelled with the *ENTRY* attribute.

identifier: ENTRY (parameterlist)

The alternative entries are called like any procedure by means of a *CALL* statement. It has been proposed, in conjunction with modular programming, that procedures with several entries should be used for realizing the data modules in PL/I.

PASCAL

```
        FUNCTIONintegral (FUNCTION f: REAL; from, to: REAL): REAL;
                local__declarations;
BEGIN       . . .
            . . . f(x) . . .
            . . .
END; {integral}
```

ADA
```
        GENERIC (FUNCTION f(x: real) RETURN real)
        FUNCTIONintegral (from, to: real) RETURN real IS local__declarations;
BEGIN       . . .
            . . . f(x) . . .
            . . .
END integral;
```

Fig. 11.7   Procedures as parameters.

Almost all programming languages accept that procedures can occur as procedure parameters. Numerical integration of a given function (Fig. 11.7) is a typical example of this type of application in the techno-scientific field. ADA

---

† The equality of two modes is a significant aspect here (see section 7.4).

forbids this, in order to be able to check the procedure calls for syntactic correctness at translation time. However, in this case, the programmer can declare a generic function name. Individual ones can then be formed by using specific functions, for example:

FUNCTION integral__h IS NEW integral(h)

12

Coroutines and processes

12.1 Incarnations

Many textbooks on programming describe the effect of a subroutine call by the copy rule: the effect of the call is the same as if the calling statement were replaced by a copy of the body of the defined procedure. (Certain language dependent substitutions must be made here for parameters and to remove any conflicting identifiers.) This interpretation only covers the classical case of a simple subroutine and leads to complications when applied to more general concepts. (1) Recursive subroutines would lead to program texts of infinite length if the copy rule is statically applied. However, a dynamic interpretation of the copy rule, in which the copy process is not invoked until the subroutine is called, can be of some help. (2) If the procedure is not started by a statement occurring explicitly in the program, then it is not obvious at which point the procedure body should be copied. This is the case with procedures initiated by interrupts. (3) The copy rule assumes that the procedure is always restarted at the beginning rather than continued from the point at which it was interrupted in an earlier call. This applies for coroutines. (4) It is also based on the premise that the calling program is not further processed as long as the called program remains unfinished. This means that one single deterministic instruction sequence exists; simultaneous or shared processing of both programs as concurrent processes is not possible. (5) The called program is started directly by the call. One alternative would be to regard the call as an instruction to be carried out at a later point in time.

A clearer concept is obtained by regarding the declaration of a procedure as a pure definition and distinguishing it from the executable incarnation. The definition simply fixes what is to be done. Each call creates a new incarnation corresponding to the declared frame. In this case, recursive calls differ from non-recursive ones only in that the newly created incarnation matches algorithmically one that already exists, whereas the data in the new incarnation differs in general from that in earlier ones. Hence, an independent data set, which contains the return address in particular, is attached to each incarnation.

Using this model, cases which cause problems when applying the copy rule can be handled. (1) Recursive subroutines ensure that several incarnations exist simultaneously (the dynamic copy rule would be adequate here too). (2) The creation of incarnations can be done independently of the program run by means of events that occur. (3) The incarnation does not necessarily have to be erased when the program run leaves it—it can exist further and be later continued. (4) Several incarnations of different or the same procedure can be processed together concurrently. (5) The creation of an incarnation and the start of processing does not have to be done by the same statement but can be carried out independently.

The above description assists in interpreting the meaning of reentrant procedures. These are, in fact, procedures which are called by a process within a system of parallel processes, even though the call within another process is not terminated. Both processes then use different incarnations of this procedure. As this situation cannot be ascertained at translation time, the compiler must either translate all relevant procedures as reentrant or the programming language must provide for the procedures in question to be suitably labelled. SIMULA is an example of the former alternative: all procedures within classes are translated as reentrant. PL/I uses the second alternative: all such procedures must be identified as *REENTRANT*.

As the algorithm is the same, the same statement sequence can be used for all incarnations, but using different data. If the implementor wishes to keep the statement sequence in the computer just once, he must avoid all statements which change the program or allow direct access to variable objects. Addressing mechanisms, which allow an exchange of data when changing from one incarnation to another, must be chosen.†

12.2 Coroutines

The function of coroutines is to allow equal collaboration between two or more procedures. In contrast to the classical subroutines, coroutines can remain 'alive' even after control has been passed from the routine. When the next call comes, they continue from the point at which they were abandoned the previous time. Fig. 12.1 shows a simple example in which a main program creates two coroutines which then operate alternately for a time.

The concept is based on the assumption that two different call statements and two different return statements exist. *CALL* statements are required to create the incarnation which usually directly causes the initial start, and for subsequent continuation from the point at which the called coroutine was last abandoned. One of the return statements keeps alive the incarnation for subsequent continuation and the other one provides a final shutdown in which the incarnation is erased. In Fig. 12.1, this final return statement is always assumed at the

---

† The base registers provide a way of implementing this satisfactorily.

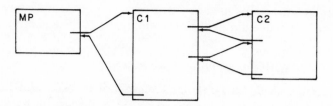

Fig. 12.1 Simple example of the interplay between two coroutines, *C1* and *C2*, created and started initially by a main program *MP*.

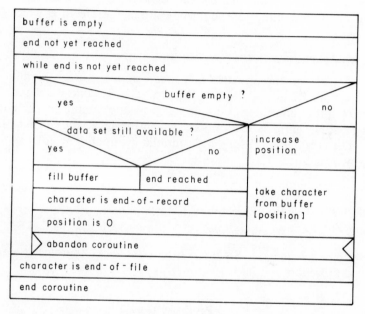

Fig. 12.2 Example of a coroutine (input buffer administration).

end, whereby logical rather than physical end of the procedure is meant. Fig. 12.2 gives a standard example for coroutines, i.e. the administration of an input buffer.† Each time the coroutine is abandoned, the next character from a sequential input file is assigned to the variable *character*. On re-entry, the coroutine is continued after the statement responsible for the abandonment—in this instance with a renewed repetition of the *FOR* range— as long as the end condition for the *DO* loop is not satisfied.

The coroutines of SIMULA are class incarnations (procedures can again be declared based on the nesting principle). Accordingly, the declaration takes the form:

CLASS classidentifier (formal_parameter);
    specification_of_parameter

---

† See chapter 14.

This determines the frame used in the construction of the individual incarnations, which is initiated during the program by the *NEW* statement:

incarnationidentifier
  :- NEW classidentifier (parameter)

The parameters provide for a different initialization of the incarnation-specific data, which in the case of the example in Fig. 12.2, includes the buffer size and the identification of the file to be read, but can also cover the specification of the identifiers of other coroutine incarnations with which they should cooperate. Before the incarnation can be created, its identifier must be declared, and information must be given regarding the references which should be allowed.

REF (classidentifier) incarnationidentifier

SIMULA works on the principle that incarnation is started initially by the actual creation. Return to the creating procedure is done via the statement *DETACH* if the coroutine is to be subsequently continued. In contrast, reaching and executing the statically last statement signals the end of this incarnation. The creating procedure can continue a coroutine which has already begun, by means of

CALL (incarnationidentifier)

Change from one coroutine to another is done by

RESUME (incarnationidentifier)

Both continue statements in SIMULA offer no chance of parameter passing to the called procedure.

12.3 Processes (tasks)

The coroutine stands between the classical procedure on the one hand and the software process (task) on the other. Whereas continuation and abandonment of an incarnation is always effected by an explicit statement in coroutines, a process can be suspended or continued in other ways, e.g. by the occurrence of specific events. The task, on the execution of an incarnation on a computer system, is a special case of the more general process concept as defined by DIN 66201: a system of interacting processes by which material, power, or information is transformed, transported, or stored. The lifespan of a task begins with its creation and ends with its deletion. This deletion can be done by the task itself or caused by another task. As only language constructs which are provided by the higher-level programming languages are being considered here, the so-called second mode tasks, which are characterized by the fact that they are subject to a uniform central task administration, are of primary importance in this context. (First mode tasks are started by an interrupt or supervisor call and do not relinquish the processor voluntarily.)† The necessity of this type of task

---

† Further details will be found in textbooks on operating systems.

administration is shown by the fact that tasks should be continued on the occurrence of previously defined events (as the task is not operating, it cannot enquire whether the event has occurred) and that in general in a computer system more tasks are available for simultaneous processing than there are processors available. It makes no difference whether the tasks belong to completely independent jobs or whether several tasks within a program are in joint collaboration.

A basic model for the task states can be derived from the above-mentioned problems. Fig. 12.3 depicts the model from an operating system viewpoint. According to this, at any point in time, each task is either current, ready, or waiting. Current (active) means that the task has a processor which allows the execution of its statements to be continued.† If all conditions for the start or continuation of a task are satisfied but no processor has been made available by the task administration, then it is said to be ready. The third case is when the task itself cannot be continued even if a processor is available. It is waiting for an event to happen (it is blocked). This event may take the form of a specific operating state from another task, a point in time, an external signal, or the allocation of resources.

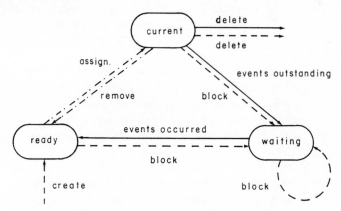

Fig. 12.3   Model showing states for second-mode tasks.

On closer consideration, these three states can be further sub-divided. For example, SIMULA or PEARL use a model with two waiting states; Ammann (1980) has provided a diagram to illustrate this. The VDI/VDE draft specification 3554‡ distinguishes as many as five waiting states for process FORTRAN. (1) The task is known as activated when it is waiting only for missing resources. (2) In the 'waiting for time' state, it can be activated at a specified point in time. (3) If the task is waiting for an event, then it is activated when that event actually occurs; in this context, an event simply means an interrupt. (4) If the task is in the 'locked' state, then it can only be activated upon a corresponding statement from another task. (5) The final category is 'dormant', in which case the task

---

† Interruption by first mode tasks is of no importance here.
‡ March 1978 version.

exists but has not yet started; the start occurs when it is moved to one of the other waiting states by another process.

12.4 State transition

Fig. 12.3 showed the state transitions which are possible between the individual states. These state transitions can be caused in different ways. There are those induced by the task itself and those which can be caused also or only by other tasks. Statements in the programming languages are required for both of these cases. However, the state transitions between 'ready' and 'current' occur only as the responsibility of the process administration; there are no statements in the program to correspond to these transitions.

The task administration selects one of the waiting processes when a processor becomes free. This task thus becomes current.† The criterion for selection varies. Tasks are often assigned priorities, whereby the one with the highest priority is next in line. Another criterion selects the task which has been in the 'ready' position the longest. This can also be used as an additional factor when tasks of the same level of priority are waiting. If a task with a higher priority than the current one becomes ready, the latter is interrupted, removed from the processor by the task administration, and put back into the ready state. The processor is now available for handling the task of higher priority. Another allocation strategy is time slicing, in which a processor is made available to each ready task for a specified time interval only; after this time interval has elapsed, the task is replaced by another, which is similarly given a specified time. None of these various displacement operations changes the processability of the task in the least. From a task point of view, all these strategies have a similar effect. Hence textbooks on the respective programming languages do not elaborate on this.

The task itself can only trigger state transitions when it is in the 'current' state as a statement must be executed for this purpose. It can either terminate it or convert it to the 'waiting' state. There are various reasons for this transition, but they can all be summed up by the fact that an event is outstanding provided the event concept has been defined along sufficiently broad lines. Waiting for the end of input/output requirements, for the release of a resource taken up by another task, or simply for a specific time are all suitable examples. If the event for which the process is waiting occurs, it is not put back into the 'current' state but into the 'ready' state. It becomes processable once again and competes with other such tasks for a processor. The transition is only indirectly triggered by the task itself in that it does in fact determine the events to which a reaction will take place. Thus, these transitions arise explicitly in the program.

If a task is affected by another task, then the corresponding statements obviously appear in the latter and can only be carried out when it is in operation. This means that transfer of a current process to the waiting state by means of another task is only possible in a multi-processor system. In contrast to this,

---

† In a single-processor system, only one task can be in the 'current' state; a multi-processor system can obviously involve many.

a ready process can be transferred to the waiting state in a single-processor system, too. In both cases, the blocked task does not execute the statement specifying the event for which it will become ready again. For this reason, either the blocking task must determine this event together with blocking (e.g. time) or a task must explicitly suspend the block. Either the blocking task or a third task can do this. A special case arises when a task waiting for a self-defined event is blocked by another one as well. In this instance, the occurrence of the original event is not sufficient to make the process ready. A deblocking operation must occur and this is one of the reasons why the waiting state can be further subdivided.

12.5 State transition statements

Two cases can be distinguished for state transition formulation at the level of problem oriented programming languages: the language constructs required for both task description and administration can be realized as a standard procedure call (or even by interspersed assembler instructions) or the language may contain its own language constructs for this purpose. Process-FORTRAN (VDI/VDE 3554) and CORAL 66 (Depledge, 1976) belong to the first group and PL/I, PEARL (Kappatsch *et al.* 1979), ADA (Ichbiah *et al.* 1979), plus languages such as Concurrent PASCAL (Brinch Hansen, 1975), and MODULA (Wirth, 1977) which are not as popular but have widespread influence on language development, belong to the second.

The implementation of a task requires some measures to be taken to ensure that the program describing the task is identified in a special way. This is done by the declaration which appears as follows in PEARL:

identifier: TASK [*priority*] [*RESIDENT*] [*GLOBAL*];
 body

The *RESIDENT* option can be used to establish that the task is not pushed out of the main storage even in the waiting state. The identifier may also be classified to be global and a priority may be assigned to the tasks thus described. In PL/I, the task can be declared like any normal procedure, because it is clear from the context that the call

CALL identifier (parameter) TASK

or

CALL identifier (parameter) EVENT

relates to a task. In ADA, the task declaration is distinguished from the module declaration by the word symbol *TASK* alone.

The creation of a concrete incarnation by the process administration, which is tied up with the initial start in the languages covered here, must be distinguished from the declaration. In PL/I, this is done by the above mentioned *CALL* statement, in PEARL the statement is *ACTIVATE*, and in ADA it is *IN-ITIATE*. One special aspect of ADA is that a statement can create an array of incarnations:

INITIATE indentifier (subscript__bounds)

The termination of a task occurs either when the physical or logical end is reached (*RETURN* statement) or by the use of special cancel statements: *ABORT* in ADA, *TERMINATE* in PEARL. These can be applied either to the actual task or to others. However, in the latter case, the identification of these other tasks must be given. PL/1 incorporates the *STOP* statement, which not only stops the operating task but also the one which had created it.

The synchronization statements described in the next chapter, and the input/output statements which mostly place the task in the waiting stage belong to the group of statements which cause state transitions. There are also explicit statements for state transition. PEARL uses the *SUSPEND* statement which places the task being performed in the waiting state without giving a concrete event for which it must wait. It can only be 'woken up' by another task; this is done by a *CONTINUE* statement. If the task has placed itself in the waiting state and specified an event which will cause its continuation, it can be further blocked by another task which prevents the occurrence of the specified event; PEARL uses the *PREVENT* statement for this. Fig. 12.4 gives a review of such statements.

ACTION	PL/I	PEARL	ADA	PROCESS-FORTRAN[1]
Start (by others)	*CALL*	*ACTIVATE*	*INITIATE*	*START TRNON CYCLE TCYCLE CON*
Wait	*WAIT*	*SUSPEND RESUME*[2] *REQUEST*	*DELAY* [4]	*WAIT HOLD*
block (by others)	-	*PREVENT*	[4]	-
release	*OCCURRENCE OF ANTICIPATED EVENT*			
release (by others)	[3]	*CONTINUE*	[4]	*RELSE*
end[5]	*RETURN STOP*	*TERMINATE*	*ABORT*	*STOP*
end (by others)	-	*TERMINATE*	*ABORT*	*CANCL UNCON*

Fig. 12.4   State transition statements.
1   All statements are *CALL* statements.
2   Together with appointing a time.
3   Can be achieved via *COMPLETION(eventparameter) = 1*.
4   Implicit in the rendezvous technique.
5   Apart from reaching the physical end.

Waiting for fixed points in time is very important in real time applications. This is another instance in which the various languages have different degrees of flexibility. PEARL is the language selected by way of example here. There are three alternatives to be considered for a primitive schedule: (1) an absolute moment (*AT time*) which is independent of the time of schedule execution, (2) the moment at the end of a given timespan (*AFTER duration*) which is calculated from the time of schedule execution onwards, and (3) a moment determined by an external event (*WHEN interrupt*). Apart from these primitive schedules which can also be used in combination, there are also periodic ones

ALL duration

or

ALL duration UNTIL time

or

ALL duration DURING duration

These can only be used in the *ACTIVATE* statement.

13

Synchronization of parallel tasks

The problem with software tasks operating in parallel is that they must be synchronized. At first glance, there seem to be two cases in which synchronization is required: firstly, when resources are being shared, and secondly, when waiting for specific points in the tasks.

If resources are shared (data, program parts, hardware resources), it must generally be ensured that, at any point in time, only one task has access to any particular resource. Hence, while a process has access to a resource, any further access attempts must be excluded. For example, if a task modifies data, then another task which reads this data at the same time would under some circumstances be supplied with inconsistent values. Dijkstra proposed his semaphore variables to define locking and releasing operations by way of a solution to this problem back in 1968. Later, integer semaphore variables, capable of blocking further access after a prescribed number of locking operations, were introduced for the case of a resource which is available for a finite number of concurrent accesses.

In the case of a task not being able to be pursued until another one has reached a specific point, it does not matter whether the process is a software task or a technical process. Synchronization is achieved by sending and then awaiting a message. The literature refers to signals or the occurrence of events, according to perspectives. However, this is just a different way of formulating the same ideas.

Despite the fact that the objectives of the two cases are different at first glance, along with the primitive operations derived from them, an equivalence is easily found. For example, release and locking semaphore operations can be simulated by sending or awaiting messages. The problem in applying these primitive synchronization operations is the same as that encountered with control structures: they can lead to obscure synchronization structures in which the presence (and removal) of deadlock situations is difficult to check. A deadlock occurs in a system of tasks when no task can be handled further because each one is waiting for a message from another task. The following cross-over access is an example: task p has ensured access to data a and awaits the release of data b; however, this is in the possession of task q, which for its part is awaiting the release of data a. Hence, more clearly arranged algorithms can be better achieved by proceeding to higher-level compound structures in the synchronization field too.

13.1 Semaphore variables

The Boolean semaphore variables can accept the values *free* and *occupied*. The two operations with which they can be examined or modified are normally designated by P and V.† $P(s)$ tests whether s is occupied and if so places the requesting task in the waiting state; conversely, if s is free, it is then marked as being occupied and the requesting task can be continued. $V(s)$ releases s; if other tasks have made requests in the meantime and are waiting, one of them can then be continued. However, P and V must always be regarded as atomic statements although they are composed of many instructions. If s were in the free state and a further request was made between the test and the subsequent value change, this would also come across a free s, and both tasks would be continued. Therefore, hardware support is essential if these operations are to be effectively implemented.

The description of the P and V operations shows that a synchronization mechanism consists not only of the two statements, but also a counter and a queue: the counter makes the decision as to whether inquiring tasks can be answered, and the queue accepts all processes for which the access request could not yet be fulfilled.

If a program part wants to access specific resources exclusively (i.e. no other program part is allowed to access the same resources at the same time), a semaphore variable is assigned to these resources and the program part is embraced by a $P-$ and a $V-$ operation. Fig. 13.1 shows this concept for a buffer, used jointly by several tasks, where some tasks enter data and some read data. Access to the buffer and its data is protected by the statements *REQUEST* and *RELEASE*. This solution is certainly easier to understand than the one given in Fig. 13.2, but has a distinct disadvantage: when the buffer is full, the task represented is not put in the waiting state at the next attempt to write, but remains in a loop in which it will always inquire again whether the buffer has empty positions available (active waiting). This permanent access to the buffer hinders other tasks wanting to read from it.

The solution given in Fig. 13.2 overcomes this disadvantage by preserving access to the buffer for the writing task only if at least one position is free, otherwise it is placed directly in a waiting state. This is achieved by using integer semaphore variables. They permit a prescribed finite number of access attempts, and are suitable for use with resources which will be available more than once. The inquiring task can be continued if the semaphore variable is

---

† *P*roberen (test) and *V*rijgeben (release).

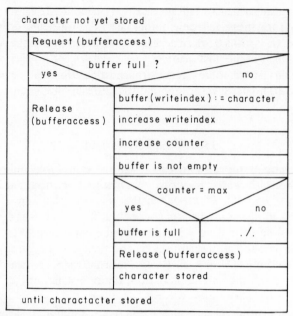

Fig. 13.1   Entries made in a common buffer with PEARL operations. The reading task is formulated in the same way.

DECLARE   *buffer (max) CHARACTER,*
               bufferaccess SEMA PRESET (1),
               empty SEMA PRESET(max),
               full SEMA PRESET(0),
               writesubscript, readsubscript FIXED INIT 1;

write: *PROCEDURE (symbol CHARACTER) REENT;*
                  REQUEST empty;
                  REQUEST bufferaccess;
                     buffer (writesubscript) := symbol;
                     writesubscript := MOD (writesubscript,max) + 1;
                  RELEASE bufferaccess;
                  RELEASE full;

END;

read: *PROCEDURE RETURNS CHARACTER REENT;*
                  DECLARE symbol CHARACTER;
                  REQUEST full;
                  REQUEST bufferaccess;
                     symbol := buffer(readsubscript);
                     readsubscript := MOD (readsubscript,max) + 1;
                  RELEASE bufferaccess;
                  RELEASE empty;
                  RETURN (symbol);
END;

Fig. 13.2   Writing into and reading from a common buffer with integer semaphore variables.

positive; at the same time it is reduced by *1*. The *V* operation causes an increase of *1*. In the example in Fig. 13.2, the actual value of the semaphore variable *empty* indicates how many of the buffer positions are free. A writing task lowers the value using the *P* – operation *REQUEST*† and increases the value of the comparable semaphore variable *full* after entry is terminated. Reading tasks work conversely.

An example is formulated in PEARL, which allows integer semaphore variables:

DECLARE identifier SEMA [PRESET (expression)]

The *P* – function *REQUEST (identifier)* and the *V* – function *RELEASE (identifier)* provide access to the semaphore variable declared in this way. ADA incorporates Boolean semaphore variables within the framework of a standard task. In PL/I, the *LOCK* and *UNLOCK* statements, in the context of files, or the *EXCLUSIVE* attribute correspond to this concept.

13.2 Events

Two states can also be distinguished for events: the event has occurred or it has not yet occurred. There are differences relating to the position in the program at which a reaction takes place, whether the occurrence of events can be programmed explicitly and how many tasks are affected by the event.

An event can be triggered explicitly by a program statement, i.e. the task may reach a specific program position or a prescribed state. To a certain extent, this event can be identified as expected, because its occurrence depends on the progress of an algorithm. The alternative is the unexpected event, which bears no relationship to any specific point in the algorithm. Interrupts caused by hardware can be put into this category. In a similar way, a distinction can be made as to whether the reaction to the occurrence of an event takes place at a known point explicitly mentioned in the program or is unanticipated. The reaction can be explicitly determined by a waiting operation: by calling this operation, the task suspends itself until the event occurs, as long as it has not already taken place. The synchronization effect is obvious. A reaction with no reference to the actual state of processing can be initiated by means of the exception handling discussed earlier. A note must also be made as to whether the occurrence of an event of this type affects only one or all of the waiting tasks. Languages such as MODULA and ADA activate only one task, whereas a PL/I event will activate them all. PEARL allocates programmed signals to the first group and interrupts to the second.

The question as to whether the program is working correctly is best overlooked if both event creation and the reaction to it take place at well defined points in the program. In *MODULA* for example, this is done by *WAIT* and *SEND* instructions: *WAIT(event)* suspends the calling task until the event occurs. If it has already occurred, the calling task can be continued and, as far as further

---

† If the two *REQUEST* statements at the beginning of the procedure are exchanged with each other, this could lead to deadlock under adverse circumstances.

requests are concerned, that event has not happened. *SEND(event)* means that the event occurs and one of the tasks awaiting this event can be continued. The event variables are declared in MODULA as *SIGNAL*.

The PL/I events are similar in structure. When a task is started, an event can be assigned to it:

CALL task EVENT (event)

and this remains at a value of *0* as long as the task is in operation. On termination its value is *1*. The request can be made by

WAIT (list_of_events) [(number_of_anticipated_events)]

When the specified number of events has occurred, the requesting task is continued.† According to the definition, no explicit *SEND* statement is required because the event is set when the logical end of the task is reached. The possibility of working with events not allocated to a task also exists, these are declared by

DECLARE a EVENT

and modified by

COMPLETION(a) = 0 or COMPLETION(a) = 1

PEARL signals are linked with specific instructions during which they can occur and this depends on implementation. They can be raised by *INDUCE* statements, which are mainly used for simulation purposes, during the test phase and cause subsequent exception handling. PEARL interrupts are also dependent on implementation. In contrast to the signals, an interrupt affects all tasks which allow reaction to this interrupt. If there should be no reaction, this can be achieved by the statement

DISABLE interruptidentifier

and switched on by

ENABLE interruptidentifier

The reaction to an interrupt must be ascertained by a scheduling statement (*WHEN*).

Out of all the languages covered, only PL/I specifies that one of several events must be awaited, without saying exactly which one it should be. In the other languages, this must be simulated. This can be done by allocating an auxiliary task to each possible event. The task then waits for the event to happen and release a general semaphore variable. All the actual task in question has to do is await this semaphore variable release.

13.3 Monitor

The monitor concept was devised by Brinch-Hansen (1975) and Hoare (1974) and incorporated in PASCAL and Concurrent PASCAL. It is essentially based

---

† If there is no second bracket, all of them must occur.

on the class concept of SIMULA: each monitor consists of data which it has to administer, and access procedures which are available to the user. In association with data module requirements, the data to be administered are not known by the user so that access to them is via the monitor procedures only. Various tasks can call the monitor procedures and each of these then runs as part of the calling task. However, only one task at a time can use procedures of the same monitor. In this way, the monitor can obey the principle of mutual exclusion when handling common resources (Wirth, 1977b).

The common use of a buffer by several tasks, which was discussed earlier, is described by a monitor in Fig. 13.3. If a writing task comes up against the statement *wait(nonfull)*, then it must wait until a reading has released a position in the buffer and signalled this by means of *send(nonfull)*.

```
INTERFACE MODULE buffer__administration
        DEFINE write, read;
        VAR    buffer: ARRAY 1 .. max OF character;†
               write subscript, read subscript, counter: integer;
               nonfull, nonempty: signal;
        PROCEDURE write (symbol: character);
        BEGIN
               IF counter = max THEN wait (nonfull) END;
               buffer [write subscript] : = symbol;
               write subscript : = write subscript MOD max + 1;
               counter : = counter + 1;
               send (nonempty)
        END write;
        PROCEDURE read (VAR symbol: character);
        BEGIN
               IF counter = Ø THEN wait(nonempty) END;
               symbol : = buffer [read subscript];
               read subscript : = read subscript MOD max + 1;
               counter : = counter - 1;
               send(nonfull)
        END read;
        BEGIN
               write subscript : = 1; read subscript : = 1;
               counter : = Ø
        END buffer__administration
```

Fig. 13.3   Writing into and reading from a buffer by means of a monitor.

13.4 ADA rendezvous

This differs from the monitor concept in that the data to be administered and the administration itself combine to form a separate task. Operations on the data are therefore not done as procedures which when called become part of another task. A more detailed examination shows the rendezvous to be unsym-

---

† *max* denotes a constant.

```
TASK buffer__ administration IS
      ENTRY read (symbol: OUT character);
      ENTRY write (symbol: IN character);
END;
TASK BODY buffer__ administration IS
      max:           CONSTANT integer : = concrete__ value;
      buffer:        ARRAY (1 .. max) OF character;
      write subscript, readsubscript: integer RANGE 1 .. max : = 1;
      counter:       integer RANGE 0 .. max : = 0;

BEGIN
      LOOP
            SELECT WHEN counter < max = >
                              ACCEPT write (symbol: IN character)
                              DO       buffer(write subscript) : = symbol;
                              END;
                              write subscript : = write subscript MOD max + 1;
                              counter : = counter + 1;
                  OR WHEN counter > 0 = >
                              ACCEPT read (symbol: OUT character)
                              DO       symbol : = buffer(read subscript);
                              END;
                              read subscript : = read subscript MOD max + 1;
                              counter : = counter − 1;
            END SELECT;
      END LOOP;
END buffer__ administration;
```

Fig. 13.4   Writing into and reading from a buffer by means of an ADA rendezvous.

metrical: the administration waits for requests from other tasks. These are *read*
and *write* in the example of Fig. 13.4:

ENTRY request(list__of__formal__parameters)

Mutual exclusion during access to common resources is achieved because the
administration task has well-defined positions each of which controls a request:

ACCEPT request(list__of__formal__parameters) DO
        if required, sequence of statements which are executed with mutual
        exclusion
END

If a task requests a service, then it is suspended until the administration task
reaches the corresponding *ACCEPT* statement. The statements provided are
then carried out and the requesting task continued when the *END* allocated to
the *ACCEPT* has been reached.† Should the administration task reach an
ACCEPT statement and no suitable request be present, it is suspended.

In most applications, requests do not come in a fixed sequence and the
administration task has to wait for one of several possible requests. ADA pro-

---

† The fact that the subscripts and counter have not been updated at this point in time does not lead
to any inconsistency, as only the administration task has access to these.

vides a *SELECT* statement for this:

SELECT first__request__with__handling;
OR   second__request__with__handling;
OR . . .
[ELSE statement sequence]
END SELECT

In this case, the administration task reacts to an alternative for which a request is available. Should none be present, then the statements in the optional *ELSE* section are carried out provided this option exists. In the example shown in Fig. 13.4, the requests *write* and *read* are awaited as alternatives.

These alternatives are incorporated in a loop so that, when a request is processed, all requests then become possible once more. There is no *SELECT* statement in Fig. 13.5; hence the requests are dealt with in the given sequence. This means that the *P* operations cannot be accepted again until an *V* operation has been carried out.

The example with the buffer given in Fig. 13.4 shows that there are situations in which a request cannot be processed. For example, nothing more can be written in a full buffer. Conditional requests can be used to overcome this situation:

WHEN condition => ACCEPT request

Fig. 13.5 shows that the ADA rendezvous has the same effect as using semaphore variables. Signals can also be simulated in the same way.

GENERIC TASK semaphore IS
            ENTRY p;
            ENTRY v;
END semaphore;
TASK BODY semaphore IS
BEGIN
            LOOP ACCEPT p;
                 ACCEPT v;
            END LOOP;
END semaphore

Fig. 13.5   Simulation of semaphore variables by means of the ADA rendezvous.

14

Input and output

Previous chapters have dealt with the elements which make up a program and with which a program operates. However, a program is only meaningful if it is supplied with data from an external source and/or communicates results to the outside world. The outside world is regarded as everything which does not belong to the program.

Input statements are used for reading the data, i.e. for transporting them into the storage area allocated to the program. The source of this data may be an input device in its strictest sense (e.g. punch card reader, keyboard used in dialogue operations, analogue-digital converter, telecommunications), a peripheral storage medium (such as magnetic tape or disk), or a file held in the computer itself. Conversely, results can be communicated to the environment by output statements. Apart from the output devices as such, (printers, punch card units, display screens, digital-analogue converters, telecommunications), the writing process is also aimed at the peripheral storage media and internal computer files. The last two groups are especially suitable for communication between various programs.

Programming languages differ greatly in their concept of input/output statements, and the intended application plays a major role in this respect. Input and output are only of minor importance in the processor intensive applications in the techno-scientific field. Only convenient input and clear output format is required. Considerable amounts of data are processed in the commercial and administrative fields and structure, order principles, and access mechanisms play a very decisive role. In process control, data often arises in a non pre-determined order and with varying degrees of importance.

14.1 Model for the input/output process

As with all other programming language structures, it makes no sense to adapt the input/output statements to the technical specifications of equipment already available. It is much better to establish a model concept for the I/O process which will cover as wide a range of units as possible. In the early days of programming languages, this concept was of no special importance, so that the I/O statements in FORTRAN and COBOL mirrored the punchcard structure or line structure of the printer.

Two aspects dominate the thinking behind the current model: (1) I/O units are considerably slower than the processor so that the program has to wait at each transaction. (2) The amount of data read by one instruction is dependent on the equipment and must be prepared accordingly for output. At programming language level, neither the waiting time nor the portioning nor the equipment-related size of the portions should be made explicit in the statements. This is achieved by inserting two buffers in each input and output process (Fig. 14.1): from the input device, the data are carried over into a buffer, record by record, under the control of routines specially adapted to the equipment (equipment drivers). The size of the buffer corresponds to the physical records of the device. At the other end of the model, at the program level, logical records with size and structure oriented towards application purposes are defined. The language-specific I/O routines are a buffer of corresponding length. Conversion between the two buffers is required to summarize several physical records into one logical one, or divide one physical into several logical ones.† The output process proceeds in exactly the reverse way.

The concepts of file and record are central to the understanding of an I/O model abstracted from the special properties of the equipment and, as already mentioned, a distinction must be made between the logical side at program level

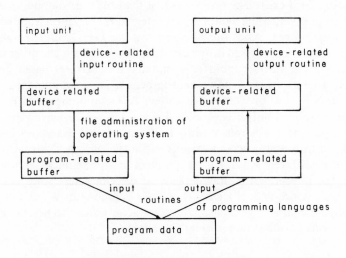

Fig. 14.1   Model for the input/output process.

---

† The two buffers can physically coincide (saving a transport process). In this case they are distinguished only by different pointers.

128

and the physical side at machine level. A record means a sequence of symbols (bytes) or bits, whereas a file is a sequence of records.† As the symbols also consist of individual bits, the difference must be precise: records are said to consist of symbols such as those of a commonly used code (e.g. ASCII). Thus, in principle, these files are machine independent.‡ As seen earlier, numbers must be translated between external and internal representations. If this translation process is not carried out when transferring data to a peripheral storage medium, then the records will consist of a sequence of binary, machine-dependent represented values and are known as binary files.§

The contents of a punch card or print line represent a simple example of a physical record. With magnetic disks, the sectors of a track, whole tracks, or cylinders (i.e. overlying tracks of the various disks in a file) can assume the record function. In contrast to the examples named so far, the length of a record is not fixed on a magnetic tape and can be arbitrarily selected. Records of variable length are also often found in input data via a terminal, where an input line can be regarded as a record irrespective of length; in this case, the carriage return functions as a termination character. In most cases of process control, the physical record consists of only a very few bytes or bits.

14.2 Various types of data transfer

Whereas the machine-related I/O routines always process a complete record, the other end of the model is not tied to the machine environment at all. This means that the programming languages can contain statements for both record-based data transfer (at logical record level) and a character-based one. In record-based data transfer, only statements for undivided input or output of a logical record exist. The program must then offer a compound object (array, record) into which the values are transferred for input or from which they are taken for output. After the whole record has been read, the individual components can be processed in any order. In line with this, the order in which data are entered in the output buffer is immaterial. Character-based data transfer is made up of a stream of individual characters. The predominant concept here is that each is read or written separately; this simply means in reality that the program-related buffer is processed character by character. The most important aspect of this is that it leads to the successive characters being not only assigned in the program to various variables 'on input' but also being interpreted in different ways, e.g. as numbers or alphanumeric characters. In this case, the interpretation may depend on the characters read just prior to the character concerned. Statements or their components which not only handle individual characters but also allow character groups to be combined to standard mode constants are normally available.

---

† Consideration of logical records gives a logical view to the files, and the same applies for the physical side.
‡ Obviously, this only happens when no machine-based file labels are used.
§ Standard FORTRAN 77 uses the notions formatted and non-formatted; however, we cannot subscribe to this.

The problem as to whether data forming a logical record must be read in, or written out, within a single statement (e.g. FORTRAN, PL/I) or can be distributed over several (e.g. SIMULA) is treated differently by the various programming languages. A special record advance instruction is required for the latter case.

If an object is formed from a group of characters, then the format of this representation is important: for example, a real value constant can be represented externally as a fixed point or floating point number and the decimal point put in various positions. In many cases, explanatory comments are useful and the ability to choose freely the spacing between numbers is important. If the layout required by the output or expected by the input statement can be determined within certain limits by the programmer himself, we will call this edited data transfer. Some language descriptions call this formatted data transfer (as opposed to format-free data transfer), but we do not favour this terminology because non-edited output data are also formatted using a so-called standard format.

There are also I/O statements in which the programmer can have no special influence on the layout: an object mode-related standard format is chosen for the output and the constants to be read in are identified by their individual phenotypes themselves. This non edited data transfer presupposes, for example, a sequence of constants clearly separated from each other (comma, blank space) for the input. Otherwise, they may be arbitrarily written within the framework of the normal syntax rules.

Both modes have their advantages and disadvantages. Preparation of input data for nonformatted statements is much easier than that for the formatted ones as there is no tiresome counting of positions, length of text strings, or blank spaces to be done. However, text strings must be incorporated within special delimiter characters as a general rule. On the other hand, a layout which is tabulated and adapted to the problem is possible in editing statements.

14.3 Input/output statements

Statements which bring about the input and output of data are dealt with differently by the various programming languages. In the majority of cases, these statements are of a typical form and are introduced by a special key word. On the other hand, in the ALGOL family, they are regarded as procedures and are thus subject to appropriate rules. APL and SNOBOL have a rather special form in which input and output are handled by so-called pseudo-variables.

Various general points can be discussed irrespective of whether the external form is a special statement or procedure. The input statement requires one or more variables to which the values read in are assigned. In addition to enumerating all the variables, some programming languages allow whole arrays or records either by itemizing their identifications or by special loop-lists. If compound objects are named as the storage area, then as many values are read in as the number of corresponding object components, in accordance with their declaration. The output statement thus requires variables with defined values. In addition to the possibilities offered by the input, it is good policy to allow

Language	Keyword	Editing	Identification of I/O medium	Data lists	Control information in statement
FORTRAN 77	*READ* *WRITE* *PRINT*	format given	integer variable	yes	formats, exceptions (separate)
PL/I	*GET* *PUT*	*EDIT:* yes *LIST:* no *DATA:* no	file identifier[1]	yes	formats, record control *COPY*
	READ FILE *WRITE FILE*	no		record transfer	exceptional access key
BASIC	*READ* *INPUT* *LINPUT* *WRITE*	no	integer variable[2]	yes	-
	PRINT	yes			format (USING)
COBOL	*DISPLAY* *ACCEPT*	no	device identifier	no	-
	READ *WRITE*	yes	file identifier[1]	record transfer	exception -
PASCAL	*READ* *WRITE*	no	file variable[1]	yes	record advance[3]
SIMULA	*INtype*[4] *OUTtype*[4]	no yes	file variable[1]	no	(separate)

Fig. 14.2 Input/output alternatives in various languages.
1 A file is to be assigned to each device.
2 Lack of these for *READ* means an internal file filled with *DATA*, otherwise output device.
3 *READIN, WRITELN*.
4 Special procedures for each object mode: *ININT, INREAL*, etc.

expressions to be evaluated and the result to be then printed out. Control information is also required to regulate the input and output statements. This may be wholly or partly compulsory, optional, or fixed once and for all as part of the language definition or implementation. Fig. 14.2 shows the most significant I/O variations in the different languages.

The extent of control information in an I/O statement depends on the facilities offered to the programmer. Essential control information includes specification of the device or file to which the statement is oriented and establishment of format in the case of formatted statements.†

Devices or files can be determined by identifiers or numbering. FORTRAN 66 and BASIC use numbers exclusively (channel numbers), but integer variables may occur in their place. The I/O medium is then identified by the numerical value last assigned to these variables; this provides a certain flexibility

---

† In FORTAN 77, the specification as to whether the statement is formatted or not is done by the presence or absence of the format specification; in PL/I, another key word is used.

as the same program can pick up another I/O medium after changing the parameter. PL/I and COBOL identify files and devices by identifiers. Languages such as PASCAL and SIMULA also incorporate file variables. Identification of the I/O medium is not necessarily available in all programming languages but in these cases standard media are predefined.

Further control information covers exception handling.‡ Writing and reading errors play a part in this. An attempt to extract more data from a record than is contained in it, or to read further records at the file end may be regarded as an example. If exception handling is specified within the I/O statement (FORTRAN 77), then it obviously refers to that alone. In contrast, PL/I incorporates separate language constructs for exception handling, which can also be used for universal application. The *COPY* specification in PL/I which allows the data read in to be printed again without the need for any special output statement, is a special case.

PL/I and FORTRAN are examples of languages in which several I/O steps can be combined in one statement. The data for transfer is given in a data list. A simple specification, in which the individual list elements may be of totally different types, is sufficient in the first instance:

PUT EDIT (sum, 3∗x + 2, 'diff = ', y − x) (format—list)

The connection between the individual elements of the data list and the format list is given by their sequence. However, it is useful to be able to write data lists in which the number of elements is an unknown factor when the program is drawn up, especially when dealing with the input and output of arrays. Hence, in PL/I and FORTRAN, a loop specification is incorporated in the data list (implied do):

(data—element DO loop—specification)

In this way,† the I/O process is repeated with the prescribed data element, and with the values of the loop variable, as often as indicated by the loop specification.§ The case in which the data element contains the loop variable as a subscript is an interesting one:

(matrix(i,j) DO i = 1 TO n)

Moreover, a data element is formed by bracketing, thus providing the opportunity for nested loop specifications. In PL/I, the same effect can, of course, be achieved by incorporating the input or output of the data element in a loop statement. However, in FORTRAN there is a difference due to the fact that each I/O statement begins a new record and hence each data element itself forms a record.

14.4 Formatting

SIMULA is taken as an example of the input and output possibilities offered by

---

‡ See section 10.6.
† PL/I language used in these examples.
§ See section 10.3.

the ALGOL family. There are three classes to which the I/O statements are allocated as procedures: *INFILE* for input files, *OUTFILE* for output files (both operate sequentially) and *DIRECTFILE* for files which can be both read from and written to; *PRINTFILE* and *PUNCHFILE* are special categories of *OUTFILE*. The output procedures are formatted in so far as they require the number of positions as a parameter. This can be given by an arithmetic expression and thus can be made dependent on the actual program data:

OUTINT(x, number__of__digits)
OUTREAL(x, digits__after__point, total__characters)
OUTFIX(x, digits__after__point, total__characters)
OUTTEXT(textconstants)

In the last case, the number of characters is given by the text constant length. The text function *BLANKS(number)* is provided for producing blank spaces.

SIMULA makes explicit use of the buffer model: if a record (line) has been composed by using these statements, it is transferred to the file by *OUTIMAGE*. The pointer within the buffer is handled implicitly by the I/O statements but can also be changed explicitly by *SETPOS(position)*.

Files or devices in the *INFILE* class are dealt with in exactly the same way. A further procedure for the *DIRECTFILE* class is given by positioning the file on an arbitrary record by means of *LOCATE(record__number)*. The *PRINTFILE* class incorporates additional procedures for controlling the page format.

PL/I and FORTRAN do not restrict the formatted process specifications to the number of digits. As they combine several I/O processes in one statement, several format specifications must be combined to give a format list. An output statement in PL/I, for example, may appear as follows:

PUT EDIT (datalist) (formatlist)

The most important elements used to make up the format list are:

F(w,d)	for decimal fixed point numbers,
E(w,d)	for decimal floating point numbers,
A(w)	for text constants,
X(w)	for blank spaces,

where w is generally an arithmetic expression giving the number of characters. As a rule, w is greater than the number of digits, as the decimal point, sign, and exponent (in the case of floating point numbers) have all to be taken into consideration. d gives the number of digits after the decimal point.† Control specifications, as given below, may also be incorporated into the format list:

COLUMN(column__number)
LINE(line__number)
PAGE	for beginning a new page
SKIP	for beginning a new line.

LINE, PAGE, and *SKIP* can also be used outside the format list.

---

† A shift in the decimal point from its actual position is achieved by incorporating a third parameter.

If individual formats or parts of format lists are to be used several times in the same statement, they can be provided with a replication factor placed before the format or bracketed list:

(COLUMN(10), F(6), 3(X(4), A(3), E(16,8)), 2F(6,1))

Format handling in FORTRAN is exactly the same. Apart from notation, there is a difference in that only integer constants can be used for the number of digits.

Apart from the nonformatted statements *DISPLAY* and *ACCEPT*, COBOL uses record data transfer as a basis for I/O.

READ filename RECORD INTO identifier.
WRITE recordname FROMidentifier.

COBOL makes a distinction between working storage section and file section. As a unique mapping is achieved between I/O files and I/O media in the declaration, the source and location of the transfer can be determined by file or record name alone.† The optional *INTO* or *FROM* permits direct transfer to or from the working storage area: after reading the record into the input area, a direct value assignment to the working storage area is given by the identifier. Conversely, the *FROM* option extends the *WRITE* statement such that a value assignment is given to the output area in the first instance. Apart from these options, the programmer can provide for data transfer between I/O and working storage area at any arbitrary position in the program, by using the statement *MOVE*.‡

The declaration of I/O areas is no different from the declaration of data structures in the working storage area.§ Formats automatically emerge from the detailed description of the individual components displayed. Columns which may be disregarded are labelled by the pseudo-selector *FILLER*.

The above-mentioned assignment of an I/O area to a file is carried out in the file declaration by the clause

DATA RECORD IS identifier.
DATA RECORDS ARE list of indentifiers.

The second form of this declaration can be used by the programmer to allocate several input areas to the file. These are of different structure and are all filled by the input statement. After a request for a distinctive component has been made, further processing can make use of either one structure or the other. These constructions are essential when records with different structures occur in the same file. There will be no discussion here of whether this is reasonable from a programming methodology point of view. In PL/I, the differently structured components of the record are assigned to a variable declared as a character string during the input process.† When a decision has been made on the format to be used, there is a new 'read-in process' in which the final target

---

† Asymmetry may be disregarded (see next section).
‡ The *READ FILE* and *WRITE FILE* instructions in PL/I work in the same way.
§ See section 7.3.
† FOTRAN 77 has adopted this concept.

variables and the final formats are used only at this point. The character string variable now functions as a source:

GET STRING (characterstring) EDIT (datalist) (formatlist)

14.5 Special features

APL and SNOBOL incorporate only a very rudimentary input and output and regard them as a special form of value assignment. SNOBOL provides the pseudo-variables *INPUT* and *OUTPUT* for this purpose and APL uses the pseudo variable □. If the pseudo-variable occurs on the right side of a value assignment, or generally within an expression, then the next value for reading in is used. In APL this is a standard mode constant or an array, and in SNOBOL it is a line whatever the composition. When the pseudo-variable occurs on the left side of the value assignment, the value on the right side is printed out. One APL example is □ ← *4* + □ *∗2*. In this case, 4 is added to the square of the input value and the result is printed out.

Assignment of constants read in by an input statement to the internal program variables is generally done in sequence: the constants which are read in are assigned to the variables occurring in the input statement in the given order. Hence, when preparing the input data, the program user must know the sequence in which program data are required. PL/I offers a 'data-controlled' input statement as an alternative.† This involves reading an input text consisting of value assignments, thus establishing not only the new values, but also the target variables to which these values are to be assigned. Hence the variable list in the input statement becomes superfluous and may be omitted. A simple example can be used to clarify the point: if we have an input text

t = '*test_no.5*', a = *3.5*, $z(1,1)$ = *4*, $z(1,4)$ = *5;*
t = '*test_no.6*', a = *4.0*, $z(1,1)$ = *6*, $z(2,3)$ = *− 8; . . .*

then the first *GET DATA* statement means that the variables a and t and the two specified array components of z are changed, whereas all other variables and array components retain their original values. In the next *GET DATA* statement, further reading takes place after the semicolon concluding the first input.

14.6 File modes

As we have seen, data transfer between a program and files can be character or record based; it is not essential that these files are such in the true sense of the word (in accordance with the file administration used by the operating system), they may be other types of I/O data handled as files. Other aspects cover transfer direction, access mode, and physical properties. When considering transfer mode a distinction must be made between input files (*INPUT*), output files (*OUTPUT*), and files which can be both read from and written to (PL/I: *UPDATE*, COBOL: *I–O*). For many applications, records are processed in a

---

† There are FORTRAN compilers which offer this facility but do not correspond to the standard.

given order—pure input or output files (sequential files) fall into this category. However, random access to records makes sense especially for record oriented transfer to and from *UPDATE* files (*DIRECT* in PL/I). Additional specifications, e.g. on the type of address, supplement the file description: record searching by key information, index-sequential storage, etc. It would be too much to discuss all the possible formulations which PL/I and COBOL have to offer here. A systematic representation of the structure and use of files would fill a whole book in itself. Reference should be made to the various books written on the subject for the different languages.

14.7 Environment description in COBOL

The assignment of file identifications to peripheral devices is just one way of linking the program with its environment. COBOL incorporates a series of other possibilities and summarizes them in the environment division. As this program component is highly dependent on concepts specified by the manufacturer of the system, and on possibilities afforded by the actual installation, just a simple example will be used here by way of explanation, (Fig. 14.3). This not only specifies a certain computer type, but also lays down a specific memory size necessary for regular program operation. The device identified in the program as a *printer* must match that identified by the manufacturer as *OUTPUT* and the file *customer-list* is assigned to it.

```
ENVIRONMENT DIVISION.
CONFIGURATION SECTION.
SOURCE-COMPUTER. cyber.
OBJECT-COMPUTER. cyber MEMORY SIZE 32000 WORDS.
SPECIAL NAMES.
        OUTPUT IS printer.
INPUT-OUTPUT SECTION.
FILE-CONTROL.
        SELECT customer-list ASSIGN TO OUTPUT.
```

Fig. 14.3   Example of a COBOL environment description.

14.8 Data stations and system division in PEARL

Process control languages must be able to describe data transfer to and from the technical process. Apart from data which are also transferred during other applications, interrupts and signals play a very important role. PEARL attempts to combine these various components into an object with a higher abstraction level, by using the object mode *DATION* (i.e. data station). This type of object consists of up to four channels. The data channel picks up the data to be transferred and is always incorporated. The control, interrupt, and signal channels are optional. The control objects correspond to the format lists in other languages and serve as an interface control; during data transfer, each corresponds to an element of the data list (matching control) or may affect the internal state of the interface (non-matching control). The object declaration

DECLARE run CONTROL (BIT(1)) MATCH FLOAT GLOBAL;
DECLARE location CONTROL MATCH FLOAT GLOBAL;
DECLARE (carriage_ error, run_ error) SIGNAL GLOBAL;
DECLARE carriage DATION INOUT FLOAT
              CONTROL (run, location)
              SIGNAL (carriage_ error, run_ error) GLOBAL;

Fig. 14.4   Declaration of a working carriage at program level (algorithmic section).

carriage, used for carriage control by means of a stepping motor, is given by way of example (Fig. 14.4).† This declaration enables all details regarding stepping motor control to be kept out of the problem-based algorithm. The position of the carriage can be read by a statement such as

READ position FROM carriage BY location

in the algorithmic part of the program.

The task of the environment description (system division) is to describe the interface to the physical process. To this end, the data stations which are specifically required must be selected after those forming part of the hardware environment and problem-related identifications must be assigned to them. A simple device specification is enough for standard devices, but more detailed linkage regulations are demanded for all other instances. These describe the linkage between data stations or data station arrays. One example is given here out of the many possibilities available (Fig. 14.5). This is based on the assumption that the significant output data for the stepping motor in the example runs via terminal positions $\emptyset-3$ in the 18th module of a CAMAC rack 1.‡ Feedback is via the interrupt terminal *IRPT(18)* and a negative acknowledgement is carried out via the signal terminal *SIGN(100)*.

The components of the internal program data stations formulated at the higher level (Fig. 14.4) must be converted into the concrete stages represented in Fig. 14.5 in order to communicate with the outside world. PEARL clarifies this process by using the data path concept, which can pass through several data stations of different abstraction levels under certain circumstances and along which the required interface conversion can take place. These interfaces are tasks which receive messages by the I/O statements. They remain in existence even when there are no instructions for processing and can react to interrupts. Fig. 14.6 describes the interface between the system description and the algorithm. It is clear from this that, in addition to the two data stations being connected, all the valid I/O statements which apply to both must be described. In this case, many variants, amongst them the *READ* statement can be defined; *location* is the only variant given in the example.

---

† Part of a more extensive research program carried out as a thesis by Schedelbeck at the Institute for Mathematical Machines, and Data Processing at Erlangen-Nürnberg University, in which ADA and PEARL were compared.
‡ CAMAC = standardized process peripherals.

$CAMC*1 < - > CRT (1)*18 - > POS(18);$
$\qquad\qquad POS(18)*\emptyset \rightarrow crorder:;$
$\qquad\qquad POS(18)*1 \rightarrow leftcarriagestop: howfast:;$
$\qquad\qquad POS(18)*2 \rightarrow rightcarriagestop:;$
$\qquad\qquad POS(18)*3 \rightarrow crreadysignal:;$
$SIGN(1\emptyset\emptyset) \leftarrow negative\_\,acknowledgement:;$
$IRPT(18) \leftarrow position\_\,reached:;$

Fig. 14.5   Declaration of the system division of a working carriage.

carriage interface:
INTFAC (carriage DATION INOUT FLOAT
$\qquad\qquad$ *CONTROL (run, location)*
$\qquad\qquad$ *SIGNAL (carriage__ error, run__ error)*
$\qquad$ *(crorder*
leftcarriagestop, howfast,
rightcarriagestop,
crreadysignal) DATION OUT BASIC
$\qquad\qquad$ *INTERRUPT (positionreached)*
$\qquad\qquad$ *SIGNAL (negative__ acknowledgement)*
$\qquad$ *) GLOBAL;*
READ: ENTRY;
$\qquad$ *location: ENTRY;*
$\qquad\qquad$ *RETURN (position);*
$\qquad$ *END; /∗ location ∗/*
END; /∗ read ∗/
... /∗ further procedure declarations follow ∗/
END; /∗ end of carriage interface ∗/

Fig. 14.6   Interface between the system description and the algorithm.

Conclusion

At the end of a book such as this, the author is never very happy—he sees all the gaps but recognizes that compromises are needed if the book is to be kept to a reasonable size. Neither system implementation languages nor dialogue aspects are covered here (only the algorithmic core of dialogue languages such as APL has been discussed). The importance of file handling and the programming language formulation of process peripherals certainly warrants a much more detailed representation ....

In many parts of the book, the various language constructs have been assessed from a modern programming methodology viewpoint. However, the comment made on this subject by someone at a meeting (ACM SIGPLAN Not.12, 1 (1977), p.1) should never be overlooked:

'A poor programmer can generate bad code in any language.'

References

Aho, A.V., and Ullman, H.D. (1972) *The Theory of Parsing, Translation and Compiling*, Vol. 1, Englewood Cliffs, NJ: Prentice-Hall.

Aho, A.V., and Ullman, H.D. (1973) *The Theory of Parsing, Translation and Compiling*, Vol. 2, Englewood Cliffs, NJ: Prentice-Hall.

Albrecht, R., et al. (1973) *BASIC*, New York: Wiley.

Alefeld, G., et al. (1972) 'Einführung in das Programmieren mit ALGOL 60'. In *Hochschultaschenbücher,* Vol. 777. Mannheim: Bibliographisches Institut.

Allen, J.R. (1978) Anatomy of LISP, New York: McGraw-Hill.

Ammann, U. (1980) 'Vergleich einiger Knozepte moderner Echtzeitsprachen'. In *6. GI-Fachtagung Über Programmiersprachen und Programmentwicklung (Darmstadt, March 1980)* H.-J. Hoffmann (ed.), *Informatik-Fachberichte*, Vol. 25, Berlin: Springer, pp. 1–18.

Andersen, C. (1964) *Introduction to ALGOL 60*, Reading, MA: Addison-Wesley.

Armstrong, R.M. (1973) *Modular Programming in COBOL*, New York: Wiley.

Backus, J.W. (1960) 'The syntax and semantics of the proposed international algebraic language of the Zürich ACM-GAMM Conference', In *Proceed. Internat. Conf. Informat. Processing (Paris, Jun. 1959)*, München: Oldenbourg, pp. 125–132.

Backus, J.W. (1978) 'The history of FORTRAN I, II and III', *ACM SIGPLAN History of Programming Languages Conference (Los Angeles, Jun. 1978) ACM SIGPLAN Not. 13*, **8**, pp. 165–180.

Bauer, F.L., and Goos, G. (1971) 'Informatik—Eine einführende Übersicht' In *Heidelberger Taschenbücher*, Vol. 80 and 91, Berlin: Springer.

Bauer, F.L., and Wössner, H. (1972) 'The 'Plankalkül' of Konrad Zuse: a forerunner of today's programming languages'. *Communicat. Associat. Comput. Mach. 15*, **7**, pp. 678–685.

Becker, H., and Walter, H. (1977) *Formale Sprachen*, Braunschweig: Vieweg.

Blatt, D.W.E. (1980) 'On the great big substitution problem', *ACM SIGPLAN Not. 15*, **6**, pp. 19–27.

Böhm, C., and Jacopini, G. (1966) 'Flow diagrams, Turing machines and languages with only two formation rules', *Communicat. Associat. Comput. Mach. 9*, **5**, pp. 366–371.

Bowles, K.L. (1977) *Problem Solving Using PASCAL*, New York: Springer.

Brauch, W. (1979) *Programmieren mit FORTRAN*, Fourth edition, Stuttgart: Teubner.

Brinch Hansen, P. (1975) 'The programming language Concurrent PASCAL', *IEEE Transact. Software Engineering 1*, **2**, pp. 199–207.

Brooks, R.E. (1980) 'Studying programmer behaviour experimentally: the problems of proper methodology', *Communicat. Associat. Comput. Mach. 23*, **4**, pp. 207–213.

Chirlian, P.M. (1973) *Introduction to FORTRAN IV*, New York: Academic Press.

Chomsky, N. (1956) 'Three models for the description of language', *IRE Transact. Informat. Theory IT-2*, **3**, pp. 113–124.

Chomsky, N. (1959) 'On certain formal properties of grammars', *Informat. Control 2*, pp. 137–167.

Dahl, O.J. (1968) 'Discrete event simulation languages'. In *Programming Languages* F. Genuys (ed.) London: Academic Press, pp. 349–395.

Dahl, O.J., and Hoare, C.A.R. (1972) 'Hierarchical program structures'. In *Structured Programming* O.J. Dahl et al. (eds.) London: Academic Press, pp. 175–220.

Dahl, O.J., and Nygaard, K. (1968) 'Class and subclass declarations'. In *Proc. IFIP Working Conf. on Simulation Languages (Oslo, May 1967)* J.W. Buxton (ed.) Amsterdam: North-Holland. pp. 158–174.

Denert, E., and Franck, R. (1977) *Datenstrukturen*, Mannheim: Bibliographisches Institut.

Denning, P.J. (ed.), (1974) 'Special issue: programming' *ACM Comput. Surveys 6, 4.*

Depledge, N. (1976) 'CORAL 66—a practical high-level language for mini-computer and application program and development', In *Real-Time Software* J.P. Spencer (ed.) Maidenhead: Infotech International, pp. 673–684.

Deransart, P. (1979) 'The language LISP does not exist?'. *ACM SIGPLAN Not. 14*, **5**, pp. 24–27.

Dewar, R.B.K. et al. (1979) 'Programming by refinement, as exemplified by the SETL representation sublanguage', *ACM Transact. Programming Languages Systems 1*, **1**, pp. 27–49.

Dijkstra, E.W. (1962) *A Primer of ALGOL 60 Programming* New York: Academic Press.

'Draft proposed ANS FORTRAN' ANS Committee X3J3 (eds.) *ACM SIGPLAN Not. 11*, **3**.

Falkoff, A.D. et al. (1964) 'A formal description of system 360'. *IBM Syst. J. 4*, **4**, pp. 198–262.

Falkoff, A.D., and Iverson, K.E. (1978) 'The evolution of APL'. *ACM SIGPLAN History of Programming Languages Conf. (Los Angeles, Jun. 1978), ACM SIGPLAN Not. 13*, **8**, pp. 47–57.

Fischer, M.J. (1972) 'Lambda calculus schemata'. *ACM SIGPLAN Not. 7*, **1**, pp. 104–109.

Geissler, R., and Geissler, K. (1974) *ANS COBOL—Einführung und Arbeitsbuch für die Praxis*, München: Hanser.

Geissmann, L. (1979) 'Modulkonzept und separate Compilation in der Programmiersprache MODULA-2'. *Proc. Microcomputing (München, Oct. 1979)* W. Remmele and H. Schecher (eds.), *Berichte German Chapter ACM*, Vol. 3, Stuttgart: Teubner, 98–114.

Giloi, W.K. (1977) *Programmieren in APL*, Berlin: de Gruyter.

Goodenough, J.R. 'Exception handling: issues and a proposed notation'. *Communicat. Associat. Comput. Mach. 18*, **12**, pp. 683–696.

Goos, G. (1976) 'Einige Eigenschaften der Programmiersprache BALG'. In *Proc. 4. GI-Fachtagung, Programmiersprachen (Erlangen, March 1976)* H.J. Schneider and M. Nagl (eds.), *Informatik-Fachberichte*, Vol. 1, Berlin: Springer, pp. 90–100.

Goos, G., and Kastens, U. (1978) 'Programming languages and the design of modular programs'. In *IFIP-TC2-Conference on Constructing Quality Software (Novosibirsk, May 1977)* P.G. Hibbard and S.A. Schuman (eds.) Amsterdam: North-Holland, pp. 153–186.

Griswold, R.W. (1978) 'A history of the SNOBOL programming language', *ACM SIGPLAN History of Programming Languages Conference (Los Angeles, Jun. 1978)*, *ACM SIGPLAN Not. 13*, **8**, pp. 275–308.

Griswold, R.E. et al. (1976) *Die Programmiersprache SNOBOL 4*, München: Hanser.

Gritsch, A., and Gritsch, R. (1972) *Das Programmieren von Computern*, München: Hanser.

Gross, M., and Lentin, A. (1971) *Mathematische Linguistik*, Berlin, Springer.

Güntsch, F.R., and Schneider, H.J. (1972) *Einführung in die Programmierung digitaler Rechenautomaten*, Third edition, Berlin: de Gruyter.

Guttag, J.V. (1977) 'Abstract data types and the development of data structures'. *Communicat. Associat. Comput. Mach. 20*, **6**, pp. 397–404.

Haase, V., and Stucky, W. (1977) *BASIC-Programmieren für Anfänger*, Mannheim: Bibliographisches Institut.

Harrison, M.A. (1978) Introduction to Formal Language Theory. Reading, MA: Addison-Wesley.

Herschel, R. (1974) *Einführung in die Theorie der Automaten, Sprachen und Algorithmen*, München: Oldenbourg.

Herschel, R. (1976) *Anleitung zum praktischen Gebrauch von ALGOL 60*, Sixth edition, München: Oldenbourg.

Herschel, R., and Pieper, R. (1979) *PASCAL-Systematische Darstellung von PASCAL und CONCURRENT PASCAL für den Anwender*, München: Oldenbourg.

Hoare, C.A.R. (1974) 'Monitors: an operating system structuring concept'. *Communicat. Associat. Comput. Mach. 17*, **10**, pp. 549–557.

Hommel, G. et al. (1979) *ELAN—Sprachbeschreibung, Wiesbaden: Akademische Verlagsgesellschaft.*

Horning, J.J. et al. (1974) 'A program structure for error definition and recovery'. In *Operating Systems (Rocquencourt, Apr. 1974)* E. Gelenbe and C. Kaiser (eds.), *Lecture Notes Comput. Sc.,* Vol. 16, New York: Springer, pp. 177–187.

Hosseus, W. et al. (1980) *PASCAL in Beispielen—Eine Einführung für Schüler und Studenten*, München: Oldenbourg.

Huskey, H.D., and Wattenburg. W.H. 'Compiling techniques for boolean expressions and conditional statements in ALGOL 60'. *Communicat. Associat. Comput. Mach. 4*, **1**, pp. 70–75.

Ichbiah, J.D. et al. (1979) 'Preliminary ADA reference manual', and 'Rationale for the design of the ADA programming language'. *ACM SIGPLAN Not. 14*, **6**.

Iverson, K.E. (1962) *A Programming Language*, New York: Wiley.

Iverson, K.E. (1979) 'Operators'. *ACM Transact, Programming Languages Systems 1*, **2**, pp. 161–176.

Jensen, K., and Wirth, N. (1978) *PASCAL User Manual and Report*, Second edition, New York: Springer.

Kappatsch, A. et al. (1979) *PEARL—Systematische Darstellung für den Anwender*, München: Oldenbourg.

Katzan, H. (1972) *A PL/I Approach to Programming Languages*, Philadelphia: Auerbach.

Kaucher, E. et al. (1978) *Höhere Programmiersprachen ALGOL, FORTRAN, PASCAL*, Mannheim: Bibliographisches Institut.

Kemeny, J., and Kurtz, T.E. (1970) *BASIC Programming*, New York: Wiley.

Kimm, R. et al. (1979) *Einführung in Software Engineering*, Berlin: de Gruyter.

Knuth, D.E. (1967) 'The remaining trouble spots in ALGOL 60'. *Communicat. Associat. Comput. Mach. 10*, **10**, pp. 611-618.

Knuth, D.E. (1974) 'Structured programming with go-to statements'. *ACM Computing Surveys 6*, **4**, pp. 261–301.

Knuth, D.E., and Merner, J.N. (1961) 'ALGOL 60 confidential'. *Communicat. Associat. Comput. Mach. 4*, **6**, pp. 268–272.

Kupka, I., and Wilsing, N. (1975) *Dialogsprachen*, Stuttgart: Teubner.

Kurtz, T.E. (1978) 'BASIC'. *ACM SIGPLAN History of Programming Languages Conference (Los Angeles, Jun. 1978), ACM SIGPLAN Not. 13*, **8**, pp. 103–118.

Lamport, B.W. et al. (1977) 'Report on the programming language EUCLID'. *ACM SIGPLAN Not. 12*, **2**, pp. 1–79.

Leavenworth, B.M. (ed.) (1972) 'Control structures in programming languages'. *Special SIGPLAN Session ACM Annual Conf. (Boston, Aug. 1972), ACM SIGPLAN Not. 7*, **11**.

Leavenworth, B.M. (ed.) (1974) 'Proceedings of a symposium on very high level languages', *(Santa Monica, March 1974), ACM SIGPLAN Not. 9*, **4**.

Lecht, C.P. (1968) *The Programmer's PL/I*, New York: McGraw-Hill.

Lefage, W.P. (1978) *Applied APL Programming*, Englewood Cliffs, NJ: Prentice-Hall.

Lindsey, C.H., and van der Meulen, S.G. (1971) *Informal Introduction to ALGOL 68*, Amsterdam: North-Holland.

Liskov, B. et al. (1977) 'Abstraction mechanisms in CLU'. *Proc. ACM Conf. Language Design for Reliable Software (Raleigh, March 1977), Communicat. Associat. Comput. Mach. 20*, **8**, pp. 564–576.

Marti, J. et al. (1979) 'Standard LISP report'. *ACM SIGPLAN Not. 14*, **10**, pp. 48–68.

McCarthy, J. (1978) 'A micro-manual for LISP—not the whole truth'. *ACM SIGPLAN History of Programming Languages Conference (Los Angeles, Jun. 1978), ACM SIGPLAN Not. 13*, **8**, pp. 215–216.

McCarthy, J. et al. (1962) *LISP 1.5 Programmer's Manual*, Cambridge Ma: MIT Press.

McCracken, D.M. (1962) *A Guide to ALGOL Programming*, New York: Wiley.

142

McCracken, D.M. (1967) *FORTRAN with Engineering Applications*, New York: Wiley.

McCracken, D. (1978) *COBOL—Anleitung zur strukturierten Programmierung*, München: Oldenbourg.

Menzel, K. (1980) *BASIC in 100 Beispielen*, Stuttgart: Teubner.

van der Meulen, S.G., and Kühling, P. (1974) 'Einführung in die Sprache'. In *Programmieren in ALGOL 68*, Vol. 1, Berlin: de Gruyter.

van der Meulen, S.G., and Kühling, P. (1977) 'Sprachdefinition, Transport und spezielle Anwendungen'. In *Programmieren in ALGOL 68*, Vol. 2, Berlin: de Gruyter.

Mickel, K.P. (1975) 'Einführung in die Programmiersprache COBOL'. In *Hochschultaschenbücher*, Vol. 745, Mannheim: Bibliographisches Institut.

Morris, C. (1938) 'Foundations of the theory of signs'. In *Internat. Encyclopedia of Unified Science*, Vol. 1, No. 2, Chicago: Univ. Chicago Press.

Morris, C. (1955) *Signs, Languages, and Behaviour*, New York: G. Braziller.

Murach, M. (1978) *Standard COBOL*, München: Oldenbourg.

Naur, P. (1975) 'Programming languages, natural languages, and mathematics'. *Proc. 2nd. Symp. Principles Programming Languages (Palo Alto, Jan. 1975)*, pp. 137–148.

Naur, P. (1978) 'The European side of the last phase of the development of ALGOL 60'. *ACM SIGPLAN History of Programming Languages Conference (Los Angeles, Jun. 1978), ACM SIGPLAN Not. 13*, **8**, pp. 15–44.

Naur, P. et al. (1960) 'Report on the algorithmic language ALGOL 60'. *Numer. Math.* **2**, pp. 106–137; *Communicat. Associat. Comput. Mach.* **3**, pp. 299–314.

Naur, P. et al. (1963) 'Revised report on the algorithmic language ALGOL 60'. *Numer. Match.* **4**, pp. 420–453; *Communicat. Associat. Comput. Mach. 6.* **1**, pp. 1–17.

Noble, J.M. (1969) 'The control of exceptional conditions in PL/I object programs'. In *Proc. Informat. Processing 68 (Edinburgh, Aug. 1968)* A.J.H. Morrell (ed.) Amsterdam: North-Holland, pp. 565–571.

Nygaard K., and Dahl, O.J. (1978) 'The development of SIMULA languages'. *ACM SIGPLAN History of Programming Languages Conference (Los Angeles, Jun. 1978), ACM SIGPLAN Not. 13,* **8**, pp. 245–272.

Ottmann Th., and Widmayer, P. (1980) *Programmierung mit PASCAL*, Stuttgart. Teubner.

Parnas, D.L., and Wurges, H. (1976) 'Response to undesired events in software systems'. In *2nd Internat. Conf. Software Engineering (San Francisco, Oct. 1976)*, Long Beach: IEEE Computer Society, pp. 437–446.

Pears, D. (1971) 'Ludwig Wittgenstein'. In *Taschenbuch* No. 780, München: Deutscher Taschenbuchverlag.

Pratt, T.W. (1975) *Programming Languages—Design and Implementation*, Englewood Cliffs, NJ: Prentice-Hall.

Pyle, I.C. (1981) *The ADA Programming Language*, Englewood Cliffs, NJ: Prentice-Hall.

Radin, G. (1978) 'The early history of PL/I'. *ACM SIGPLAN History of Programming Languages Conference (Los Angeles, Jun. 1978), ACM SIGPLAN Not. 13,* **8**, pp. 227–241.

Radin, G., and Rogoway, H.P. (1965) 'NPL—highlights of a new programming language'. *Communicat. Associat. Comput. Mach.* **8**, **1**, pp. 9–17.

Randell, G. (1975) 'System structure for software fault tolerance'. *Proc. Internat. Conf. Reliable Software (Los Angeles, Apr. 1975), ACM SIGPLAN Not. 10, 6* pp. 437–449.

Rechenberg, P. (1974) *Programmieren für Informatiker mit PL/I*, Vol. 2, München: Oldenbourg.

Rieger, C. et al. (1979) 'Artificial intelligence programming languages for computer aided manufacturing'. *IEEE Transact. Syst. Man Cybernet. SMC-9*, 4, pp. 205–226.

Salomaa, A. (1973) *Formal Languages*, New York: Academic Press.

Sammet, J.E. (1972) 'Programming languages: history and future'. *Communicat. Associat. Comput. Mach. 15*, 7, pp. 601–610.

Sammet, J.E. (1978a) 'Roster of programming languages for 1976–1977'. *ACM SIGPLAN Not. 13*, 11, pp. 56–85.

Sammet, J.E. (1978b) 'The early history of COBOL'. *ACM SIGPLAN History of Programming Languages Conf. (Los Angeles, June 1978), ACM SIGPLAN Not. 13*, 8, pp. 121–161.

Schärf, J. (1975) *BASIC für Anfänger*, Fourth edition, München: Oldenboug.

Schauer, H. (1977) *ALGOL für Anfänger*, München: Oldenbourg.

Schauer, H. (1979) *PASCAL für Anfänger*, Third edition, München: Oldenbourg.

Schauer, H. (1980) *PASCAL für Fortgeschrittene*, München: Oldenbourg.

Schneider, H.J. (1980) 'Comparison of interactive languages'. In *Proc. 1980 Annual Conf. SHARE European Association (Beito, Norway, Sept. 1980)*, Nijmwegen: SHARE European Association, pp. 151–163.

Schneider, H.J. (1981) 'Set-theoretic concepts in programming languages and their implementation'. In *Proc. Graphtheoretic Concepts in Computer Science (Bad Honnef, Jun. 1980)*, H. Noltemeier (ed.), *Lecture Notes Comput. Sc.*, vol. 100, Berlin: Springer, pp. 52–54.

Schneider, H.J., and Jurksch, D. (1970) *Programmierung von Datenverarbeitungsanlagen*, Second edition, Berlin: de Gruyter.

Schnupp, P. (1978) 'Ist COBOL unsterblich?' In *5. GI-Fachtagung über Programmiersprachen (Braunschweig, March 1978)* K. Alber (ed.), *Informatik-Fachberichte*, 12, Berlin: Springer, pp. 28–44.

Schulz, A. (1975) *Einführung in das Programmieren in PL/I*, Berlin: de Gruyter.

Schulz, A. (1976) *Höhere PL/I-Programmierung*, Berlin: de Gruyter.

Schwartz, J. (1975) 'Optimization of very high level languages', *J. Computer Languages I*, 2, pp. 161–194; 3, (1975), pp. 197–218.

Siebert, H. (1974) *Höhere FORTRAN-Programmierung*, Berlin: de Gruyter.

Simon, F. 'CONS-freies Programmieren in LISP unter Verwendung der deletion-Strategie'. In *4. GI-Fachtagung über Programmiersprachen (Erlangen, March 1976)* H.J. Schneider and M. Nagl (eds.), *Informatik-Fachberichte*, Vol. 1, Berlin: Springer, pp. 111–123.

Singer, F. (1972) *Programmieren mit COBOL*, Stuttgart: Teubner.

Spencer, D.D. (1974) *Anleitung zum praktischen Gebrauch von BASIC*, München: Oldenbourg.

Spiess, W.E. and Rheingans, F.G. (1977) *Einführung in das Programmieren in FORTRAN*, Fifth edition, Berlin: de Gruyter.

Stoyan, H. (1978) *LISP-Programmierhandbuch*, Berlin: Akademie-Verlag.

Wegner, P. (1979) 'Programming languages—concepts and research directions'. In *Research Directions in Software Technology*, P. Wegner (ed.), Cambridge, Ma: MIT Press, pp. 425–489.

Weicker, R. (1978) 'Neuere Konzepte und Entwürfe für Programmiersprachen'. *Informatik-Spektrum 1*, 2, pp. 101–112.

van Wijngaarden, A. et al. (1969) 'Report on the algorithmic language ALGOL 68'. *Numer. Math. 14*, pp. 79–218.

van Wijngaarden, A. et al. (1975, 1977) 'Revised report on the algorithmic language ALGOL 68'. *Acta Information 5*, pp. 236; *ACM SIGPLAN Not. 12*, 5, pp. 1–70.

Wirth, N. (1971) 'The programming language PASCAL'. *Acta Informatica 1*, pp. 35–63.

Wirth, N. (1977a) 'MODULA: a language for modular multiprogramming'. *Software-Practice Experience 7*, pp. 3–35.

Wirth, N. (1977b) 'Towards a discipline of real-time programming'. *Communicat. Associat. Comput. Mach. 20*, 8, pp. 577–583.

Wulf, W.S. et al. (1971) 'BLISS—language for systems programming'. *Communicat. Associat. Comput. Mach. 14*, 2, pp. 780–790.

Zahn, C.T. (1974) 'A control statement for natural top-down structured programming'. In *Proc. Programming Symposium (Paris, Apr. 1974)* B. Robinet (ed.), *Lect. Notes Computer Science*, Vol. 19, Berlin: Springer, pp. 170–180.

Zemanek, H. (1966) 'Semiotics and programming languages'. *Communicat. Associat. Comput. Mach. 9*, 3, pp. 139–143.

Zemanek, H. (1971) 'Informale und formale Beschreibung'. In *IBM-Symposium über Probleme bei der Definition und Implementierung universeller Programmiersprachen (Stuttgart, Sept. 1971)*; Unpublished; the reader will find some of the ideas in the following publication:

Zemanek, H. (1972) 'Some philosophical aspects of information processing'. In *The Skyline of Information Processing, Proc. 20th Anniversary Celebration of the IFIP (Amsterdam, Oct. 1970)* H. Zemanek (ed.), Amsterdam: North-Holland, pp. 93–140.

Zuse, K. (1949) 'Über den allgemeinen Plankalkül als Mittel zur Formulierung schematisch-kombinativer Aufgaben'. *Archiv Math. 1*, pp. 441–449.

Zuse, K. 'Über den Plankalkül', *Elektron. Rechenanlagen 1*, pp. 68–71.

Index